802.11 Security

Bruce Potter and Bob Fleck

O'REILLY®

Beijing · Cambridge · Farnham · Köln · Paris · Sebastopol · Taipei · Tokyo

802.11 Security
by Bruce Potter and Bob Fleck

Published by O'Reilly & Associates, Inc., 1005 Gravenstein Highway North, Sebastopol, CA 95472.

O'Reilly & Associates books may be purchased for educational, business, or sales promotional use. Online editions are also available for most titles (*safari.oreilly.com*). For more information, contact our corporate/institutional sales department: (800) 998-9938 or *corporate@oreilly.com*.

Editor:	Jim Sumser
Production Editor:	Darren Kelly
Cover Designer:	Emma Colby
Interior Designer:	David Futato
Production Services:	Nancy Crumpton

Printing History:

December 2002:   First Edition.

ISBN: 0-596-00290-4

[M]

Table of Contents

Part III. Access Point Security

Part IV.   Gateway Security

Preface

From the early days of wireless communication, the ability to transmit news, thoughts, and feelings without wires has revolutionized our daily lives. The radio broadcasts of the 1920s brought instant news and entertainment to households all over the world. The adoption of television in the 1950s added a visual aspect to the experience. CB radio made a big impact in the 1970s, allowing individuals within a limited distance to talk with each other while on the road. In the 1980s, cellular phones and pagers allowed people to be connected to their home or office no matter where they were. Now at the start of the 21st century, low-cost, high-speed wireless data networking has become a reality. Anyone can go to his or her local computer store and easily purchase wireless networking equipment that can transmit packet-based data at millions of bits per second.

Throughout the entire process, the integrity and confidentiality of the information traveling through the air has always been a concern. Who is *really* broadcasting the signal you are receiving? Is anyone eavesdropping on the signal? How can you make sure that an eavesdropper is unable to obtain useful information from the signal? These questions are not particularly important when you are watching television but become critical when you are transmitting data between military installations or making a stock transaction over the Internet using your 802.11b-capable PDA. Due to the ease with which an attacker can intercept or modify your 802.11b communications, it is imperative that you understand the risks in using a wireless network and how to protect yourself, your infrastructure, and your users.

Assumptions About the Reader

This book is aimed at network engineers, security engineers, systems administrators, or general hobbyists interested in deploying secure 802.11b-based systems. Primarily, the discussions in this book revolve around Linux and FreeBSD. However, there is a great deal of general-purpose information as well as tips and techniques for Windows users and users of firmware-based wireless access points.

The book assumes the reader is familiar with the installation and maintenance of Linux or FreeBSD systems. The techniques in the book rely heavily on custom kernel configuration, startup scripts, and general knowledge of how to configure the operating systems. We provide links and references to resources to help with these issues but do not address then directly. This book concentrates on the issues germane to wireless security and leaves the operating-system-specific installation procedures as an exercise to the user.

The reader is also assumed to be familiar with general networking concepts. The reader should understand, at least at a high level, concepts such as the OSI layers, IP addressing, route tables, ARP, and well-known ports. We feel this makes the book more readable and useful as a guide for *wireless* networks, not networks in general. Again, we attempt to provide references to other resources to assist readers who may be unfamiliar with these topics.

Scope of the Book

This book attempts to give you all the knowledge and tools required to build a secure wireless network using Linux and FreeBSD. You will be able to use this book as a roadmap to deploy a wireless network; from the client to the access point to the gateway, it is all documented in the book. This is accomplished by a two-step process. First, we talk about wireless and 802.11b in general. This book will give you a broad basis in theory and practice of wireless security. This provides you with the technical grounding required to think about how the rest of the book applies to your specific needs and situations.

The second part of this book details the technical setup instructions needed for both operations systems including kernel configurations and various startup files. We approach the specific technical setup using a "from the edge to the core" concept. We start by examining the security of a wireless client that is at the very edge of the network. Then, we move toward the core by providing a method of setting up a secure access point for client use. From there, we move even farther toward the core by examining secure configuration of the network's IP gateway. Finally, we zoom all the way out and discuss security solutions that involve many parts of the network, including end-to-end security.

Part I, *802.11 Security Basics*, provides an introduction to wireless networks and the sorts of attacks the system administrator can expect.

Chapter 1, *A Wireless World*, introduces wireless networking and some high-level security concerns. The chapter talks briefly about basic radio transmission issues such as signal strength and types of antennas. It also examines the differences and similarities between members of the 802.11 suite of protocols. Finally, we discuss the Wired Equivalency Protocol (WEP) and its weaknesses.

Chapter 2, *Attacks and Risks*, examines the types and consequences of attacks that can be launched against a wireless network. This chapter opens with a discussion of denial-of-service attacks, proceeds to man-in-the-middle attacks, and finishes with a section on illicit use of network resources.

Part II, *Station Security*, shows you how to lock down a wireless client machine such as a laptop. These chapters contain general security best practices for workstations (which are, unfortunately, rarely used). They also contain specific wireless kernel, startup, and card configuration. Finally, we provide tactics for stopping attackers on the same wireless network as well as how to audit the entire workstation.

Chapter 3, *Station Security*, discusses the general approach and concerns for securing a wireless client. This chapter provides a foundation for the five OS-specific chapters that follow it.

Chapter 4, *FreeBSD Station Security*, discusses specific concerns for securing a FreeBSD wireless client. This chapter discusses kernel, interface, and operating system configuration issues. It also presents techniques and tools for detecting various attacks and defending against them.

Chapter 5, *Linux Station Security*, discusses specific concerns for securing a Linux wireless client. Kernel, interface, and operating system configuration issues are presented. This chapter also presents techniques and tools for detecting various attacks and defending against them including a basic firewall configuration.

Chapter 6, *OpenBSD Station Security*, discusses specific concerns for securing an OpenBSD wireless client. This chapter discusses kernel, interface, and operating system configuration issues that are unique to OpenBSD. It also presents techniques and tools for detecting various attacks and defending against them.

Chapter 7, *Mac OS X Station Security*, shows how to securely configure a Mac OS X wireless client. Techniques for hardening the operating system as well as firewall configurations are presented in this chapter.

Chapter 8, *Windows Station Security*, provides a brief discussion of securing a Microsoft Windows wireless client. Basic ideas such as anti-virus software and firewall options are covered in this chapter.

Part III, *Access Point Security*, covers the configuration and security of access points.

Chapter 9, *Setting Up an Access Point*, shows how to install and securely configure a wireless access point. This chapter starts with a discussion of generic security problems occurring on most access points, especially firmware access points commonly available at computer stores. We also describe the installation and secure configuration of the HostAP drivers for Linux, FreeBSD, and OpenBSD.

Part IV, *Gateway Security*, covers the more complex issue of gateway configuration on several platforms.

Chapter 10, *Gateway Security*, discusses the general issues related to the configuration and deployment of the network gateway. The discussion in this chapter frames the concerns that will be addressed using the configuration guides of the three chapters that follow it.

Chapter 11, *Building a Linux Gateway*, provides the steps necessary to install and configure a properly secured IP gateway for a wireless network. The chapter discusses how to install the operating system and bring up all of the network interfaces. From there, firewall rules are presented with an explanation of why each rule is necessary. Finally, installation and configuration of supporting services such as DHCP and DNS are provided.

Chapter 12, *Building a FreeBSD Gateway*, is similar to Chapter 11 except the configurations and suggestions are for FreeBSD.

Chapter 13, *Building an OpenBSD Gateway*, is similar to Chapter 11 except the configurations and suggestions are for OpenBSD.

The remainder of the book covers technologies and techniques that can be used across the entire network.

Chapter 14, *Authentication and Encryption*, covers supplementary tools that can help secure wireless network traffic. This chapter examines the use of portals to control network access. Next, we examine the use of 802.1x and VPNs to secure the network.

Chapter 15, *Putting It All Together*, examines the interplay between the clients, access points, and gateways. This chapter opens with a discussion of how the users affect the architecture of the network. Finally, we attempt to look into the crystal ball and determine what the future holds for wireless security.

Conventions Used in This Book

- *Italic* is used for commands, directory names, filenames, scripts, emphasis, and the first use of technical terms.
- `Constant width` is used for IP addresses, network interfaces, partitions, and references to code in regular text.
- `Constant width italic` is used for replaceable text.
- **`Constant width bold italic`** is used for user input.

Pay special attention to notes set apart from the text with the following icons:

 This is a tip. It contains useful supplementary information about the topic at hand.

This is a warning. It helps you solve and avoid annoying problems.

Other Sources of Information

Wireless security is a dynamic field of study. It is important to know where to obtain the latest information on wireless technologies as well as information on the latest attacks. At the time of this writing, there are many standards under development that may drastically change the wireless landscape within the next few years. In addition, the features provided in each operating system are being enhanced and expanded constantly, so it is important to know how those changes impact your deployment.

More links can be found at: *http://www.dailywireless.org*.

Standards and References

IEEE 802 Standards Online is at *http://standards.ieee.org/getieee802/*.

The Wireless Ethernet Compatibility Alliance is at *http://www.wirelessethernet.org/*.

Operating-System-Specific Documentation

Linux Netfilter documentation is at *http://www.netfilter.org*.

The HostAP driver for Linux is at *http://hostap.epitest.fi*.

The FreeBSD Handbook is at *http://www.freebsd.org/doc/en_US.ISO8859-1/books/handbook/index.html*.

Mailing Lists

The bugtraq mailing list is a primary source for breaking news on software vulnerabilities. The vuln-dev mailing list occasionally has in-depth discussions on security problems with wireless networks. Both can be subscribed to at *http://www.securityfocus.com*.

We'd Like to Hear from You

We have tested and verified the information in this book to the best of our ability, but you may find that features have changed (or even that we have made mistakes!). Please let us know about any errors you find, as well as your suggestions for future editions, by writing to:

O'Reilly & Associates, Inc.
1005 Gravenstein Highway North
Sebastopol, CA 95472

(800) 998-9938 (in the United States or Canada)
(707) 829-0515 (international/local)
(707) 829-0104 (fax)

We have a web page for this book where we list examples and any plans for future editions. You can access this information at:

http://www.oreilly.com/catalog/80211security

You can also send messages electronically. To be put on the mailing list or request a catalog, send email to:

info@oreilly.com

To comment on the book, send email to:

bookquestions@oreilly.com

Acknowledgments

The authors would like to thank their editor, Jim Sumser, for his effort in making this book as clear and useful as possible. We would also like to thank him for his assistance throughout the process of writing this, including giving us the freedom to tackle the book in our own unique way.

Many insightful suggestions were provided during the review process, and we want to extend our deepest thanks to the reviewers: Bob Abuhoff, Agoussi Amon, Dave Markowitz, and John Viega.

Special thanks to Matt Messier for providing information and the firewall scripts for Mac OS X.

We would also like to thank O'Reilly & Associates for giving us the opportunity to write this book.

From Bruce Potter

I would first like to thank my wife, Heidi, and two children, Terran and Robert (who was born halfway through the writing process). They gave me the time and support needed to research and write this book. Without them, I never would have made it.

I would also like to thank the members of NoVAWireless for their expertise and never-ending pursuit of knowledge. Through technical and non-technical discussions on the mailing list, I have learned a great deal of information that helped me with this book.

Finally, I would like to thank The Shmoo Group and in particular, Adam Shand of PersonalTelco. You guys and gals have been the foundation for much of my technical work for the last few years.

From Bob Fleck

I would like to thank my parents for their encouragement and support of both my education and my exploration of computers as I grew up. Many thanks also to my uncle, Chris Fleck, who has fostered my interest in computer science since shortly after I learned to read.

The advice and knowledge of my coworkers and colleagues has been priceless. John Viega helped by guiding me through the trials of writing a book. Will Radosevich, Jordan Dimov, and Jose Nazario have all been a great help over the last few years as a source of discussions on wireless networking and security.

The community wireless networking groups around the world have made great contributions to understanding the uses of these technologies and developing interesting ways of deploying and securing 802.11 networks. I can't thank them enough for the knowledge they have collected on their websites and mailing lists. Just as important, I thank the ISPs that actively support wireless networking and cooperate with their customers to explore the new possibilities it provides.

## PART I

802.11 Security Basics

The phrase "wireless security" is considered by some to be an oxymoron. How can a system with no physical security hope to facilitate secure data transport? Well, with careful planning and configuration, a wireless network can protect itself from many types of attacks and become almost as secure as its wired counterpart. 802.11 can be deployed with various security mechanisms to provide robust, mobile, and hardened network infrastructure. In order to understand how and when to use the security tools at hand, you must first understand the underlying structure of the 802.11 protocol as well as the risks associated with deploying and using a wireless network. The following chapters will provide the basic grounding in how the 802.11 protocols work, the inherent security mechanisms it has, and how an attacker will attempt to exploit weak spots within a wireless network.

## CHAPTER 1

A Wireless World

Wireless networking is revolutionizing the way people work and play. By removing physical constraints commonly associated with high-speed networking, individuals are able to use networks in ways never possible in the past. Students can be connected to the Internet from anywhere on campus. Family members can check email from anywhere in a house. Neighbors can pool resources and share one high-speed Internet connection.

Over the past several years, the price of wireless networking equipment has dropped significantly. Wireless NICs are nearing the price of their wired counterparts. At the same time, performance has increased dramatically. In 1998, Wireless Local Area Networks (WLAN) topped out at 2Mb/s. In 2002, WLANs have reached speeds of 54Mb/s and higher.

Unfortunately, wireless networking is a double-edged sword. Wireless users have many more opportunities in front of them, but those opportunities open up the user to greater risk. The risk model of network security has been firmly entrenched in the concept that the physical layer is at least somewhat secure. With wireless networking, there is no physical security. The radio waves that make wireless networking possible are also what make wireless networking so dangerous. An attacker can be anywhere nearby listening to all the traffic from your network—in your yard, in the parking lot across the street, or on the hill outside of town. By properly engineering and using your wireless network, you can keep attackers at bay.

This chapter serves as an introduction to wireless networking and some of the high-level security concerns. Building a secure wireless network requires a wide breadth of knowledge; from the low-level aspects of radio transmission to understanding how various applications interact with the network. By understanding how all aspects of the network interact, you can safely and freely use wireless networks.

What Is Wireless?

The term *wireless* means different things to different people. In general, the term reflects any means of communication that occurs without wires. In this buzzword-compliant time, many of the following terms are synonymous with the word wireless:

- PCS
- WAP
- WTLS
- WML
- 802.11b
- Wi-Fi
- HomeRF
- Bluetooth

While all these terms mean "wireless" to some, most refer to different technologies. Personal Communication Systems (PCS) is a standard for cellular communication. Wireless Application Protocol (WAP) is mechanism of distributing data to lightweight wireless devices. Wireless Transport Layer Security (WTLS) performs for WAP the same role SSL does for web traffic. Wireless Markup Language (WML) is a lightweight markup language similar to HTML but designed to be rendered on small screens with low bandwidth use.

HomeRF and the 802.11 standards are competing wireless LAN protocols. They are analogous to protocols such as 802.3 Ethernet on wired networks. 802.11 is a standard developed and ratified by the Institute of Electrical and Electronics Engineers (IEEE). 802.11 products approved by the Wireless Ethernet Compatibility Alliance, are branded with the Wi-Fi mark to certify interoperability. HomeRF on the other hand is a standard developed by a group of corporations and lacks international recognition. Intel, one of the primary backers of HomeRF, stopped producing HomeRF equipment in late 2001 in favor of 802.11. In general, the majority of WLANs in use today are based on the 802.11 standard.

Bluetooth is another popular wireless network standard. Bluetooth networks operate on a smaller scale than a LAN. A network of Bluetooth devices is typically referred to as a Personal Area Network (PAN). Bluetooth enables personal devices such as cell phones, personal digital assistants, and watches to communicate. Bluetooth was designed to operate in small areas (about the size of a cubicle) with very low power consumption.

There are many reasons people choose to deploy a WLAN:

- Increased productivity due to increased mobility
- Lower infrastructure cost compared to wired networks

- Rapid deployment schedules
- Aesthetically unobtrusive

Wireless LANs are being deployed at a rapid rate but with little regard to security. This book focuses on wireless LANs in general and 802.11-based networks in particular and will attempt to outline strategies and implementations that you can use to deploy a secure wireless network.

Radio Transmission

Wireless networking is accomplished by sending and receiving radio waves between a transmitter and receiver. The theory behind RF data transmission can get very complicated and is outside the scope of this book. However, there are some basic concepts you should understand when you implement a WLAN.

Data Rate

A radio wave consists of electromagnetic energy. Visible light, television transmissions, and cosmic radiation are all forms of radio waves. Regardless of the type or purpose of the electromagnetic energy, these waves can be measured by several metrics. The *frequency* of a radio wave is how often the waveform completes a cycle in a given amount of time. The most common unit of measurement of frequency is the Hertz (Hz). A 1 Hz signal completes one cycle per second while a 10 Hz signal completes 10 cycles per second. Figure 1-1 shows the difference between the waveforms of a 10 Hz signal and a 1 Hz signal.

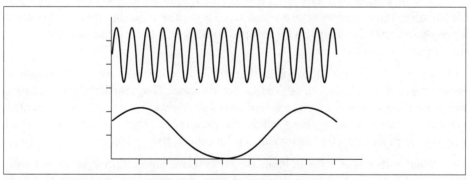

Figure 1-1. A 10 Hz signal (top) and 1 Hz signal (bottom)

Generally, the faster the frequency, the more information you can transmit and receive. The method of encoding (or *modulating*) the data affects the amount that can be transmitted. Some encoding techniques are more resilient to errors but end up with lower data rates. Conversely, high data rate modulation mechanisms may be more susceptible to outside interference.

Signal Strength

In the most general sense, the *strength* of a signal is the amplitude of its radio waveform. The unit of measurement of amplitude (or *power*) of a radio wave is a watt (W). WLAN devices typically transmit with a power of 30 milliwatts.

The strength of the signal decreases as it travels through its transmission medium—in this case, the air. This process of power loss is called *attenuation*. The amount of attenuation varies depending on the frequency of the signal and the medium through which it is traveling. *Amplifiers* can be added along a transmission medium to add strength to a signal.

The amount of power added due to amplification or removed due to attenuation is usually expressed in *decibels* (dB). Decibels provide a relative (logarithmic) measurement of signal strength. Each increase of three dB indicates a doubling in strength. Decibels are convenient because values can be added and subtracted from each other without need for complex mathematics.

While a signal is being received by a radio, the signal is also subject to noise at the same frequency as the signal. This noise may be due to environmental causes such as cosmic radiation or man-made reasons such as microwave ovens or even other radios operating in the same frequency. The ratio of the power of the received signal versus the power of the received noise is called the *signal to noise ratio* (SNR). The higher the SNR, the better the quality of the data signal.

Antennas

Antennas are critical to radios sending and receiving radio waves. They turn electrical impulses into radio waveforms and vice versa. There are hundreds of different kinds of antennas, but they can be grouped roughly into two categories: omni-directional and directional.

The name *omni-directional* implies that these antennas radiate electromagnetic energy regularly in all directions. This is not the case. They usually strongly radiate waves uniformly in two dimensions and not as strongly in the third. These antennas are effective for irradiating areas where the location of other wireless stations will vary with time like an office with many laptop computers.

Directional antennas attempt to focus the radio waves into a more constrained area. Directional antennas lack the versatility of omni-directional antennas, however they are able to utilize their power much more effectively by only emitting energy where it is needed. Directional antennas are useful for fixed location installations such as a radio connection between two buildings. As a general rule of thumb, the higher the frequency of the wave, the more transmission can be focused using a directional antenna. Figure 1-2 shows the difference in radiation patterns between an omni-directional antenna and a directional antenna.

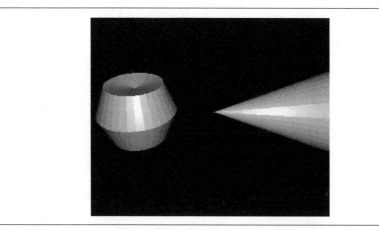

Figure 1-2. The radiation patterns of an omni-directional and a directional antenna

Sometimes antennas are deployed using *diversity*. Diversity is where a radio has multiple antennas attached to it. For a given signal, the radio decides what antenna it wants to send to and/or receive from. This allows the radio to adapt to propagation problems that may be affecting one antenna but not another. Many 802.11 PC cards have internal diversity antennas that make them more robust in hostile environments such as a typical office.

Inherent Insecurity

Data in conventional networks travels across wired mediums. Coaxial cable, twisted pairs of copper wire, and strands of fiber optics have been the foundation for networks for many years. In order to view, interrupt, or manipulate the data being transmitted, the wires or switching equipment have to be physically accessed or compromised.

An attacker does not need to physically tap into wired communication in order to eavesdrop on it. Wired communication that uses electrons to transmit data (such as phone calls and 10BaseT Ethernet) radiates small amounts of electromagnetic energy. With highly sophisticated equipment, an attacker can reconstruct the original data stream from the radiated energy. The skill required to pull off this attack as well as the relative proximity the attack requires, however, makes it highly unlikely.

Restrictions on physical access to network cables have been a cornerstone of information security. While physical protection of cables obviously does not solve all the network security problems, it helps mitigate the risk of certain man-in-the-middle (MITM) attacks. Wires are relatively easy to keep physically secure. Placing wires inside of a controlled space such as a data center keeps the physical layer secure from the majority of attackers.

When using radio frequency (RF) communication channels such as a WLAN, users lose the fundamental physical security given to them by wires. WLANs use high frequency radio waves to transmit their data. These RF waves travel through the air and are difficult to physically constrain. RF waves can pass through walls, under cracks in doors, across streets, and into other buildings. Even if a wireless access point is located inside a physically controlled data center, the wireless data may leave the bounds of the data center into uncontrolled spaces, as shown in Figure 1-3.

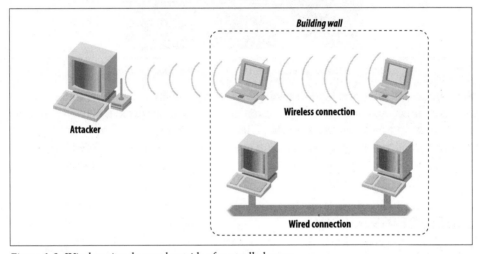

Figure 1-3. Wireless signals travel outside of controlled areas

Data on 802.11 networks can be intercepted from large distances if the attacker has line of sight. Peter Shipley, a security professional who performed some early research into wireless security, was able to eavesdrop on wireless networks in downtown San Francisco from the hills of Berkeley. That's a distance of over 20 miles! For more info on Peter's research, see his web site at *http://www.dis.org/wl/maps/*.

Due to the lack of physical control of where the wireless network data may end up, WLANs create special risks for users, administrators, and owners. Eavesdroppers many miles away may be able to intercept sensitive information or access machines that would be otherwise be protected by a firewall. When deploying a wireless network, the fundamental insecurity of the physical medium should drive the overall architecture.

802.11

Wireless networks are showing up everywhere. Corporations are deploying WLANs to allow employees to roam freely around corporate campuses without leaving the

War Driving

Attackers use many methods to gather information on computer systems that they may attack. There are automated tools to scan various networks for the existence of computer systems that may be good targets.

Before the large-scale adoption of the Internet, attackers would use automated scripts to dial large blocks of phone numbers in an effort to find modems. If the script found a modem, it would log various information about it (the number dialed, any prompt that was given, etc.), then move on to the next number. After the script was completed, the attacker could examine the output and determine numbers that may warrant further investigation. This practice of dialing in bulk became known as *war dialing*.

As the Internet gained popularity, attackers found a more efficient way to find interesting systems. By scanning large blocks of IP space for hosts and scanning those hosts for services, attackers could find weak systems to attack. This practice, known as *port scanning*, is very common and very effective.

WLANs have now become the target of mass data harvesting scripts that aim to accomplish the same goal. Using specialized software, a GPS, and a wireless-enabled laptop, an attacker can drive through a metropolitan area looking for wireless access points. The software logs varied information about the access points including latitude, longitude, and configuration. After logging all of this data, an attacker can examine the results to find a vulnerable WLAN. This practice has come to be known as *war driving*, due to its similarity to its phone-system-based predecessor.

network. Some airports offer wireless access so business travelers can be continue to be productive while waiting for plane departures. Communities are banding together to provide wireless Internet access to homes that may not have direct access to wired broadband networks.

This rapid and widespread adoption would not be possible without a well-documented and structured set of protocols. The 802.11 family of protocols provides the basis for interoperability between equipment from different vendors. A PC card that utilizes the 802.11b specification from vendor A can communicate with an 802.11b-compliant access point from vendor B.

History of 802.11

The IEEE is an internationally recognized standards setting body. The IEEE has a long history of approving and maintaining standards that set the stage for industry innovation.

The IEEE breaks their standards into various committees. The IEEE 802 Committee deals with Local and Metropolitan Area Networks. The 802 series of standards is broken into working groups that focus on specific issues within the overall discipline of LANs and MANs.

The following is a list of some of the working groups within the 802 series:

802.1
    Bridging and Management

802.2
    Logical Link Control

802.3
    CSMA/CD Access Method

802.4
    Token-Passing Bus Access Method

802.7
    Broadband LAN

802.11
    Wireless

The 802.11 Working Group was formed in September of 1990. Their goal was to create a wireless LAN specification that will operate in one of the Industrial, Scientific, and Medical (ISM) frequency ranges. The first 802.11 standard was released in 1997.

 The ISM bands are ranges of radio frequency transmission that are set aside by the FCC for low-power unlicensed operation. Cordless phones, for example, commonly use the 900 MHz and 2.4 GHz bands. Various 802.11 protocols use either the 2.4 GHz band or the 5 GHz ISM bands.

The 802 standards address the lower levels of the OSI model. However, for those familiar with the OSI layered model, the 802 series splits the data link layer into two parts: Logical Link Control (LLC) and Media Access (MAC). The 802.2 standard defines a common LLC layer that can be used by other 802 MAC and Physical Layer (PHY) standards. The most common 802-based MAC and PHY standard is 802.3 CSMA/CD Access Method, otherwise known as Ethernet.

The 802.11 protocols address the MAC and PHY layers independently. The MAC layer handles moving data between the link layer and the physical medium. It is agnostic to the currently existing PHY standards that are in deployment today. Figure 1-4 shows how the lower layers of the OSI model match up to the concepts outlined in the 802 series of protocols.

There are many different PHY standards in use today. The original 802.11 specification documented three different mechanisms: Infrared, 2.4 GHz Frequency Hopping Spread Spectrum (FHSS), and 2.4 GHz Direct Sequence Spread Spectrum (DSSS). All these mechanisms provided a 1 or 2 Mb/s data rate depending on the signal quality.

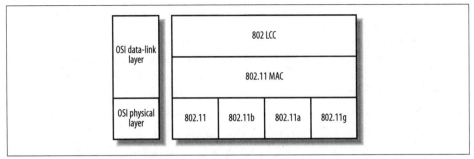

Figure 1-4. The OSI layers and corresponding 802 structure

The original 802.11 specification had low throughput and interoperability problems. A card that implemented 802.11 with DSSS could not communicate with a device that used FHSS 802.11.

802.11b, released in 1999, specified a new PHY that provided a higher bit rate using DSSS in the 2.4 GHz range. 802.11b can transmit data up to 11 Mb/s but will scale down to 1 Mb/s based on conditions. Due to the higher bit rate and increased interoperability, 802.11b has gained rapid deployment.

After the interoperability problems of the first 802.11 specification, companies in the WLAN industry banded together and created Wireless Ethernet Compatibility Alliance (WECA). WECA certifies products that use the 802.11b protocol. Their certification mark is Wi-Fi, which stands for Wireless Fidelity. A product that has been stamped with the Wi-Fi logo is certified to interoperate with other Wi-Fi devices.

802.11a, a PHY released in 2001, operates in the 5 GHz range. It provides for a bit rate of up to 54 Mb/s and uses a new modulation method called Orthogonal Frequency Division Multiplexing (OFDM). Some vendors have proprietary implementations that double the bit rate of 802.11a to 102 Mb/s.

802.11g is the fourth PHY specification from the IEEE. It operates in the same 2.4 GHz range as 802.11b but uses OFDM like 802.11a. Operating at up to 22 Mb/s, it is seen as the middleman between the 802.11b and the 802.11a standards. Table 1-1 shows the 802.11 PHY specifications.

Table 1-1. PHY specifications

802.11 PHY	Max Data Rate	Frequency	Modulation
802.11	2Mb/s	2.4GHz and IR	FHSS and DSSS
802.11b	11Mb/s	2.4GHz	DSSS
802.11g	22Mb/s	2.4GHz	OFDM
802.11a	54Mb/s	5GHz	OFDM

802.11b is currently the most deployed type of wireless LAN. Eleven separate channels can be selected for use in the 2.4GHz range. These channels actually have overlapping bands of frequencies, as illustrated in Figure 1-5. Using overlapping channels in nearby networks can cause bad interference. Most deployments have settled on using the three channels 1, 6, and 11, as this maximizes the number of non-overlapping channels available for use. Be especially aware of overlapping channels when deploying a network near the wireless LANs of other organizations; be a good neighbor, and don't interfere with the frequencies already in use around you.

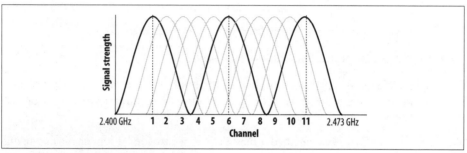

Figure 1-5. 802.11b channels

Structure of 802.11 MAC

Regardless of the underlying PHY used, the MAC is the same for all currently deployed 802.11 wireless technologies. The 802.11 MAC provides several functions: access to the wireless medium, joining and leaving a network, and security services.

Access to the wireless medium is controlled by a contention-based protocol called Carrier Sense Multiple Access with Collision Avoidance (CSMA/CA). This is a similar method to the one used in wired Ethernet. Like wired Ethernet, 802.11 devices are contending for the same physical transmission medium. If two or more devices are transmitting at the same time, their signals collide and it is impossible for the receiving station to discern the one signal from the other. CSMA/CA provides a way for 802.11 devices to probe the medium to see if it is in use and then lock the medium while they transmit.

Since 802.11 wireless networks use a shared medium, the more devices that are trying to access it, the lower the effective throughput will be. This is similar to standard wired Ethernet. When an 802.11 device is transmitting, no other device in the network may transmit data. If there are multiple devices trying to send large amounts of data, there will be heavy contention for the airwaves. This congestion gets worse as more machines are added or more data is being transmitted.

BSS and IBSS

The core unit of an 802.11 network is called a Basic Service Set (BSS). A BSS consists of a central access point (AP) and client stations. The AP coordinates all of the activities within the BSS. Due to this centralized control, BSS networks are sometimes called *infrastructure* networks. A BSS is identified by a service-set identifier (SSID). This can generally be thought of as the name of the wireless network.

A station that wants to join a BSS network will look for available APs. Some APs send beacons to inform stations of the AP's existence. Other APs suppress beacons for security reasons. Without a beacon, a station must know the SSID of the AP a priori.

Once a station has identified a BSS it wants to join, it sends an association request to the AP. The station and AP go through a handshake process that exchanges vital information regarding the network as well as any authentication that may be needed in order for the client to join the network. For more information on the authentication process, see "Authentication" later in this chapter.

Once the station has associated itself with the AP, it has officially joined the wireless network. From this point forward, the AP intermediates network communication with the station. The AP may relay traffic between two stations that are communicating with each other. The AP may also act as a bridge between the 802.11 network and a wired network such an 802.3 network.

When a station is done using the wireless network, it should disassociate from the AP. This allows the AP to clear up any internal memory it may have been using for the associated client. However, since stations may leave the network without disassociating (i.e., if a user roams out of range of the AP), APs will time out associations that haven't been used for a period of time.

In order to facilitate networks that may not have an AP to coordinate communications, an independent BSS (IBSS) may be formed between two stations. An IBSS network (sometimes called *ad-hoc*) allows two stations to associate directly with each other without an AP. While IBSS networks do not scale like BSS networks, they can be very useful for short-lived networks such as a head-to-head network game between two friends.

WEP

Interception of radio communications has been a problem for as long as radios have been used to transmit sensitive information. Radio-based communication can be used to transmit instructions to troops during warfare, credit-card info from a cell phone, or passwords from a laptop to a remote web site. Since radio transmissions travel in unsecured areas, interception of these radio signals by an attacker is a real threat. In order to protect the data from eavesdroppers, various forms of encryption have been used to scramble the data. Sometimes these encryption mechanisms have been successful; other mechanisms have been compromised, thereby subverting the security of the data.

The 802.11 MAC specification describes an encryption protocol called Wired Equivalent Privacy (WEP). The goal of WEP is to make WLAN communication as secure as wired LAN data transmissions would be. If WEP were to meet this goal, it would allow network architects to deploy wired and wireless LANs interchangeably without regard to different security risks.

WEP provides two critical pieces to the wireless security architecture: authentication and confidentiality. WEP uses a shared key mechanism with a symmetric cipher called RC4. The key that a client is using for authentication and encryption of the data stream must be the same key that the AP uses. The 802.11 standard specifies a 40-bit key, however most vendors have also implemented a 104-bit key for greater security.

Encryption

Encryption of the data stream provides confidentiality of the data transmitted between two WLAN devices. The encryption mechanism used in WEP is a symmetric cipher; this means that the key that encrypts the data is the same key that will decrypt the data. If both WLAN devices do not have the same encryption key, the data transfer fails.

When WEP is used for communication, the original data packet (P) is first checksummed (c). Then the checksum is added to the data to form the data payload. Then the transmitting device creates a 24-bit random initialization vector (IV). The device uses the IV and the shared key (K) to encrypt the data (EK,IV(P,c)) with the RC4 algorithm to create the ciphertext data. Figure 1-6 shows how a WEP encrypted packet is formed.

The device then transmits the ciphertext and the IV to the remote device. The remote device uses the IV that it received from the network and the shared key to decrypt the data and verify the checksum.

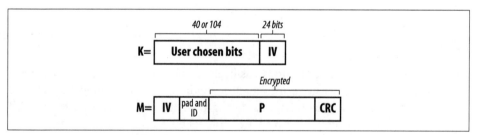

Figure 1-6. A WEP encrypted packet

Some vendors claim to have 40-bit and 104-bit encryption. Other vendors claim to have 64-bit and 128-bit encryption. 40-bit and 64-bit encryption are actually the same thing. Some vendors treat the IV as part of the key, others do not. While the IV is technically part of the key that RC4 uses to encrypt the data, it is transmitted in the clear with the packet. Therefore it is not part of the secret key. The same goes for 104-bit and 128-bit encryption.

Authentication

When a station associates with an AP, the station must authenticate itself to the AP. When the association occurs, the station and AP exchange the type of authentication they will accept. If the authentication type is specified as "open," then there is effectively no authentication. The AP and station identify themselves to each other and the association is complete.

The devices may also select the "shared secret" authentication mechanism. Station Alpha will send a *nonce* (random number) to station Beta. Station Beta encrypts the random number using WEP and sends the result to station Alpha. Station Alpha decrypts the packet and verifies the decrypted payload equals the nonce it sent to station Beta. If the numbers match, then station Alpha notifies station Beta that the authentication was successful and the association is formed.

Problems with WEP

Unfortunately, the WEP specification within the 802.11 standard does not provide wired-equivalent privacy. There are many problems with WEP that greatly reduce its advertised security.

Key Management

The WEP standard completely ignores the issue of key management. This causes problems with WLANs as the number of users grows. Using pre-shared secret keys means that every client who has the key material must be fully trusted to use that material in a legitimate way. This level of trust is not realistic. If everyone on a network uses the same key, then anyone on the network can decrypt traffic intended for any other device on the network. Also, an uneducated but otherwise trustworthy user may give the key material to another person (i.e., a friend or business associate who has stopped by the office). This new user is outside the initial trusted group of individuals who were issued the key material and could potentially compromise the network.

As the number of WLAN users grows and time passes, the amount of trust placed in secrecy of the key declines. In order to overcome this reduced trust, keys must be rotated periodically to reset the network to a trusted level. WEP provides key enumeration to allow users and administrators to rotate through a set of pre-shared keys. However, this does not drastically increase the security of the network. Instead of one key being issued to users, several keys are issued at one time. All keys are still known by the users.

Vendors are beginning to implement a per-user shared key so that each end-user device has a unique key that is shared with the access point. This protects each user from the other users on the network. By giving away their key to a friend, the only traffic they compromise is their own.

Encryption Issues

The IEEE selected 40-bit encryption because it is exportable under most national encryption laws. If the standard had only implemented 104-bit encryption, many vendors would not have been able to ship their WLAN products to other countries. Unfortunately, keys for 40-bit RC4 encryption can be found through exhaustive searching (brute force) on modern commodity PCs. A 40-bit key has just over a trillion possible values. A modern PC can search that range to find the secret key in a matter of an hour or two.

Scott Fluhrer, Itsik Mantin, and Adi Shamir released "Weaknesses in the Key Scheduling Algorithm of RC4." The paper can be found at *http://www.crypto.com/papers/others/rc4_ksaproc.ps*. In the paper, the team described a weakness in RC4 as it is implemented in the WEP protocol. The issue is not with RC4, but with the way it is used by WEP. The end result is that WEP can be cracked if enough traffic can be intercepted. Also, as the key length grows, the time it takes grows linearly. Normally as an encryption key grows, the time to break the key increases exponentially. An exponential increase would cause a key with 41-bits to take twice as long as a 40-bit key. In WEP, you need to increase the key size from 40 to 80-bits to double the time it takes to find the key. This means that a 104-bit WEP key provides no significant practical advantage over a 40-bit key. There are several freely available tools to crack WEP keys, including *AirSnort*, which can be downloaded from *http://airsnort.shmoo.com/*.

Several vendors have implemented the IV in a manner that reduces the security of WEP even further. Some vendor implementations of WEP never rotate the IV. The same IV is used for all packets sent from the client for the lifetime of the association. Other vendors rotate the IV in a predictable fashion. This allows for even faster cryptanalytic attacks.

WEP has suffered from key management problems, implementation errors, and overall weakness in the encryption mechanism. WEP may raise the bar for an attacker but provides no real security from a determined attacker. Regardless of the name,

WLANs that use WEP should not be trusted in the same way that wired networks are.

Is It Hopeless?

The wireless revolution is continuing forward, but from the picture painted so far, it may seem as if wireless networks are doomed to be large security problems. Fortunately, by understanding the risks involved in using wireless networks and properly architecting your WLAN, you can safely use wireless networks. The next step in building a secure network is understanding what an attacker can and cannot do to your network, which we'll cover in Chapter 2.

CHAPTER 2
Attacks and Risks

802.11 networks have unique vulnerabilities that make them an ideal avenue of attack. Wireless networks cannot be physically secured the same way a wired network can be. An attack against a wireless network can take place anywhere: from the next office, the parking lot of your building, across the street in the park, or a bluff many miles away.

Understanding the details of various attacks against your wireless infrastructure is critical to determining how to defend yourself. Some attacks are easy to implement but aren't particularly dangerous. Other attacks are much more difficult to mount but can be devastating. Like any other aspect of security, wireless security is a game of risk. By knowing the risks involved in your network and making informed decisions about security measures, you have a better chance at protecting yourself, your assets, and your users.

An Example Network

Throughout this book, we will work toward the creation of the example network illustrated in Figure 2-1. This network is split into three segments: the Internet, a wireless network containing access points and wireless clients, and a wired network containing workstations, servers, and other devices. A gateway mediates the traffic between these three segments. The focus of this book is the security of the gateway, access points, and wireless clients. We will also investigate the effects the security of these components has upon the rest of the network and the external security issues that originate from outside the wireless network.

All of these network components must work together, and implement complimentary security, to establish a secure network. With that in mind, we will begin by examining the classes of threats to the wireless network.

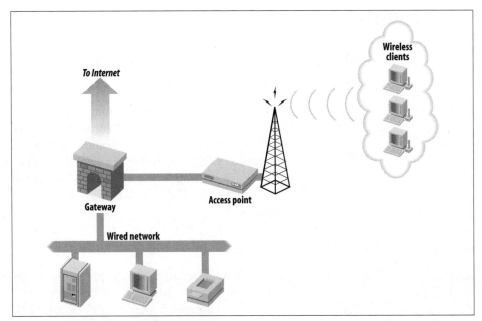

Figure 2-1. Architecture of example network

Denial-of-Service Attacks

Denial-of-Service (DoS) attacks, which aim to prevent access to network resources, can be devastating and difficult to protect against. Typical DoS attacks involve flooding the network with traffic choking the transmission lines and preventing other legitimate users from accessing services on the network.

DoS attacks can target many different layers of the network. In order to understand the risk of a DoS attack to a wireless network, you must first understand the difference between various types of DoS attacks.

Application (OSI Layer 7)

An application-layer DoS is accomplished by sending large amounts of otherwise legitimate requests to a network-aware application, such as sending a large amount of page requests to a web server, swamping the server process. The goal of this type of attack is to prevent other users from accessing the service by forcing the server to fulfill an excessive number of transactions. The network itself may still be usable, but since the web server process cannot respond to the users, access to service is denied. (This can occasionally happen, innocently, when a web site receives a sudden boost in popularity due to a link from a high-traffic site, such as *http://slashdot.org*.)

Transport (OSI Layer 4)

A transport-layer DoS involves sending many connection requests to a host. This type of attack is typically targeted against the operating system of the victim's computer. A typical attack in this category is a SYN flood. In a SYN flood (SYN packets are the first step of a TCP connection), an attacker sends an excessive number of TCP connection requests to a host hoping to overwhelm the operating system's ability to track active TCP sessions. Most operating systems have a limit to the number of connections per second they will accept and a limit on the maximum number of connections they will maintain. A successful SYN flood will overwhelm the operating system on one of these two limits, thereby denying access to the services running on that host. As is the case in the application-based DoS, the network is usually still functional, but the target host is unresponsive.

Network (OSI Layer 3)

A network-layer DoS is accomplished by sending a large amount of data to a network. This type of attack targets the network infrastructure of the victim. For example, an attacker may send 100 Mb/s of data to a network that can only transmit 10 Mb/s. The victim network obviously cannot retransmit all the data being sent to it, so the network equipment is forced to drop packets. This excessive traffic may also cause high loads on the CPUs within the network equipment itself, causing further network problems.

A typical network-based DoS attack is a ping flood. An attacker generates massive amounts of ICMP traffic destined for the victim network. (ICMP packets are used for management functions such as querying the availability and services of a host.) This usually saturates the victim's WAN links. By cutting off the victim's LAN from the rest of the Internet, the attacker has denied access to any services that reside on the victim's LAN.

Data-Link (OSI Layer 2)

A data-link DoS can target either a host or a network. Data-link attacks are launched to disable the ability of hosts to access the local network even though the hosts are still connected. An example of this would be flooding a non-switched Ethernet network with invalid frames. An attacker (or sometimes a malfunctioning NIC) can send repeated frame headers with no payload. These headers are rebroadcast to all hosts on the network and effectively tie up the medium. Data-link DoS attacks are not common on wired networks because most networking gear has the intelligence to prevent data-link attacks from propagating to hosts on the network.

Physical (OSI Layer 1)

A physical-layer DoS involves severing a host's connection to the network in some fashion. Physical attacks are not common in wired networks because they involve having direct access to the transmission medium involved in the victim's network. For instance, WAN circuits are typically buried underground and are difficult to access. LANs reside inside of buildings, making them difficult targets as well. An example of an unintentional physical DoS attack is the dreaded backhoe DoS. Backhoe attacks are common in areas of heavy construction where a large piece of equipment (like a backhoe) is digging near buried data cables. One wrong move by the backhoe operator can sever thousands of telecommunications lines, potentially taking down many services.

Wireless DoS Attacks

At the application and transport layers, there is nothing fundamentally different between DoS attacks on wireless and wired networks. However, there are critical differences in the interaction between the network, data-link, and physical layers that increase the risk of a DoS attack on a wireless network.

802.11b physical attacks

A physical DoS attack against a wired network requires very close proximity to the victim host. This is not the case with a wireless network. The medium is everywhere and attackers can launch a physical attack from much farther distances. Instead of being inside of a building to perform a physical DoS attack against a LAN, an attacker can be outside of the building. Unlike a wired network where there is usually evidence of a physical attack (destroyed cabling, removed cable, attackers on video surveillance cameras), there are no visible signs that something has changed.

The 802.11 PHY specifications define a limited range of frequencies for communication. The 802.11 devices that use a specific PHY are constrained to these frequency ranges. An attacker can create a device that will saturate the 802.11 frequency bands with noise. If the attacker can create enough RF noise to reduce the signal-to-noise ratio to an unusable level, then the devices within range of the noise will be effectively taken offline. The devices will not be able to pick out the valid network signal from all of the random noise being generated and therefore will be unable to communicate.

Creating a device that produces a lot of noise at 2.4 GHz is relatively easy and inexpensive to construct. However, there are several common commercial devices available today that can easily take down a wireless network. Unfortunately, many 2.4 GHz cordless phones that can be purchased in electronics stores have the capability to take an 802.11b network offline. While not a refined electronic weapon, these phones can interfere or completely disable a WLAN. Cordless phones use several different modulation techniques and can overlap on the frequencies used by 802.11b. This overlapping is simply noise to an 802.11b radio. The cordless-phone-induced noise can drop the SNR enough to bring down any WLAN network nearby.

> For Christmas one year, Bruce and his wife bought each other 2.4 GHz phones to replace their older 900 MHz models. After installing the phones, they noticed that they had many unexplained network outages. They also noticed an audible crackling noise on the phones. After reading the specs on the phone, they were able to set the phones to a different part of the ISM range than the frequencies they had chosen for their 802.11b network. This got rid of the interference and the outages. However, they learned the hard way that wireless technology is not necessarily plug-and-play.

There are also problems with a DoS from other networking protocols. In particular, Bluetooth uses the same ISM band as 802.11b and 802.11g. The DSSS modulation in 802.11b is susceptible to interference from the modulation used in Bluetooth networks. While there are potential solutions to prevent Bluetooth from stepping on 802.11b transmissions, large-scale Bluetooth deployments may still interfere to the point of inoperability with 802.11b networks. As time passes, the 2.4 GHz ISM band will become more crowded, making unintended DoS attacks against 802.11b networks commonplace. Sirius and XM satellite radio, who have spectrum bordering the ISM band, have complained that ISM-band devices may cause interference with their ground based repeaters and satellites

802.11b data-link DoS attacks

At the data-link layer, ubiquitous access to the medium again creates new opportunities for DoS attacks. Even with WEP turned on, an attacker has access to the link layer information and can perform some DoS attacks. Without WEP, the attacker has full access to manipulate associations between stations and access points to terminate access to the network.

If an AP is incorrectly utilizing diversity antennas, an attacker can potentially deny access to clients associated to the AP. The use of diversity antennas is intended to compensate for multi-path fade. However, diversity antennas are sometimes used to cover more area with an AP by using antennas that cover disparate physical regions.

> *Antenna diversity* is a mechanism where a single radio uses multiple antennas to overcome multi-path fade. A radio signal usually has many different paths to get to an antenna due to reflections of the signal off walls, trees, desks, etc. A radio using diversity antennas will sample a client transmission from all attached antennas and determine which antenna has the highest quality signal. The radio will then use that antenna to send and receive traffic destined for that station.

If the diversity antennas do not cover the same region of space, an attacker can deny service to associated stations by exploiting this improper setup, as shown in Figure 2-2. If diversity antennas A and B are attached to an AP, they are setup to cover both sides of the wall independently. Alice is on the left side of the wall, so the AP will choose antenna A for the sending and receiving frames. Bob is on the opposite side of the wall from Alice and will therefore send and receive frames with antenna B. Bob can take Alice off the network by changing his MAC address to be the same as Alice's. Then Bob can guarantee that his signal is stronger on antenna B than Alice's signal on antenna A by using a amplifier or other enhancement mechanism. Once Bob's signal has been detected as the stronger signal on antenna B, the AP will send and receive frames for the MAC address on antenna B. As long as Bob continues to send traffic to the AP, Alice's frames will be ignored.

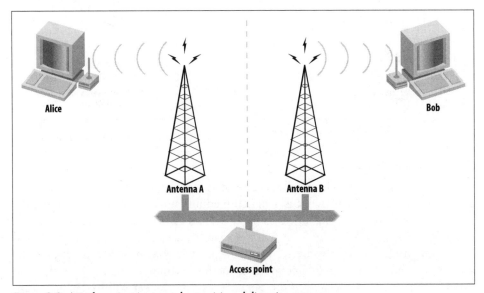

Figure 2-2. Attack against improperly provisioned diversity antennas

If a client is not using WEP authentication (or an attacker has knowledge of the WEP key), then the client is vulnerable to DoS attacks from spoofed APs. Clients can generally be configured to associate with any access point or to associate to an access point in a particular ESSID. If a client is configured to associate to any available AP, it will select the AP with the strongest signal regardless of the ESSID. If the client is configured to associate to a particular ESSID, it will select the AP in the ESSID with the strongest signal strength.

Either way, a malicious AP can effectively black-hole traffic from a victim by spoofing the desired AP. For example, if a client is configured to associate to APs in the SSID *shmoo*, the client will look for all available APs in that SSID. It will then associate with the AP for which it has the strongest signal. A malicious AP with the SSID of *shmoo* can make sure it has the strongest signal by using a larger or directional antenna, signal amplifier, etc., as shown in Figure 2-3. The client will associate to the malicious AP, and the malicious AP can drop or monitor all traffic sent to it by the client.

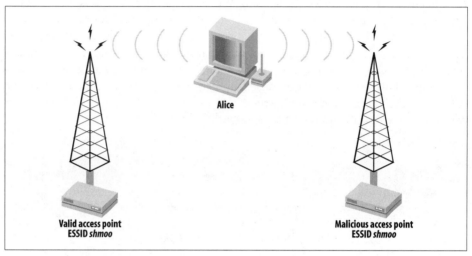

Figure 2-3. *Malicious AP overpowering valid AP*

802.11b network DoS attacks

If a network allows any client to associate, it is vulnerable to a network-level DoS attack. Since an 802.11 network is a shared medium, a malicious user can flood the network with traffic, denying access to other devices associated to the affected access point. As an example, an attacker can associate to a victim 802.11b network and send an ICMP flood to the gateway. While the gateway may be able to withstand the amount of traffic, the shared bandwidth of the 802.11b infrastructure is easily saturated. Other clients associated to the same AP as the attacker will have a very difficult time sending packets.

Given the relatively slow speed of 802.11b networks, a network DoS may happen inadvertently due to large file transfers or bandwidth-intense applications. A few bandwidth-hungry applications on a WLAN can hamper access for all associated stations. With the deployment of higher-speed WLAN technologies, these unintentional attacks will become less frequent.

Man-in-the-Middle Attacks

Man-in-the-middle (MITM) attacks have two major forms: eavesdropping and manipulation. Eavesdropping occurs when an attacker receives a data communication stream. This is not so much a direct attack as much as it is a leaking of information. An eavesdropper can record and analyze the data that he is listening to. A manipulation attack requires the attacker to not only have the ability to receive the victim's data but then be able to retransmit the data after changing it, as shown in Figure 2-4.

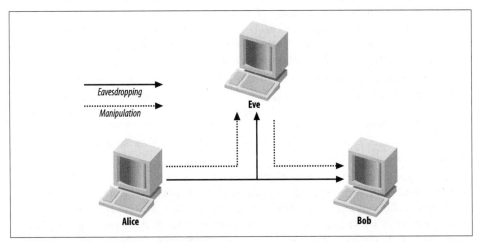

Figure 2-4. Eavesdropping versus manipulation

MITM attacks on a wired network generally require access to a network that the victim's traffic transits. This can mean physical access to a wire to "tap" into the wire for interception. It can also mean being on the same LAN as the victim and forcing traffic to go through the attacker's host. An attacker can force traffic through a malicious machine on a LAN by performing an ARP poisoning attack.

Eavesdropping

In a wireless network, eavesdropping is easy because wireless communications are not easily confined to a physical area. A nearby attacker can receive the radio waves on the wireless network without any substantial effort or equipment. All frames sent across the wireless medium can be examined in real time or stored for later examination.

Several layers of encryption can and should be implemented to obscure transmitted data in an effort to prevent attackers from gleaning useful information from the network traffic. Since the ability of an attacker to eavesdrop on wireless communications is *fait accompli*, the data-link encryption mechanism WEP was developed. If the traffic is not protected at the data-link layer using WEP, then the higher layer security mechanisms must be used to protect the data. If a security mechanism such as IPsec, SSH, or SSL is not used for transmission then the application data is available to anyone with an antenna in the area without any further effort.

ARP Poisoning

ARP (Address Resolution Protocol) is the mechanism that IP-enabled Ethernet devices use to determine which device on a network has a particular IP address. When a host wants to communicate with another host, it will send out an ARP request asking, "Who has IP address 192.168.0.1?" All hosts on the LAN receive the question, and the device that has 192.168.0.1 replies with its MAC address. The initial host then uses that MAC address to send datagrams to 192.168.0.1.

In order to reduce the number of ARP requests, many modern operating systems implement a lazy technique to learn MAC addresses. If a host receives a packet from another host on the same LAN (say, 192.168.0.1), it assumes that the MAC address on the packet is the MAC address for 192.168.0.1. It will then enter the MAC/IP address combination into its local MAC address table and use that MAC address for all future communication with 192.168.0.1.

An attacker can force packets to go through a malicious host by exploiting this lazy mechanism of learning MAC addresses. Assume an attacker wants to intercept traffic between a client (192.168.0.99) and a server (192.168.0.1). The attacker and both target hosts are on the same network. The attacker sends an ARP reply packet to the client machine with a source IP of the server but with a source MAC of the malicious machine. The client machine now thinks that the server has the MAC address of the malicious machine and will send all frames for 192.168.0.1 to that host. Conversely, the attacker sends a packet to the server with a source IP of the client and a source MAC of the malicious machine. As in the client's situation, packets will be forwarded to the malicious host.

At this point, the attacker can watch, drop, forward, and manipulate data moving between the client and the server. Even in a switched environment, this attack is successful because the switch has no way of recognizing something is wrong.

Bob Fleck and Jordan Dimov wrote a paper available at *http://www.cigitallabs.com/resources/papers/download/arppoison.pdf* that discusses how this kind of ARP poisoning can be used on a wireless network. A wireless attacker can use ARP poisoning to pull packets "off-wire" by poisoning the ARP caches of two wired hosts behind an AP. A wireless attacker can intercept traffic between any hosts on the same broadcast domain, regardless if they are wired or wireless by using ARP poisoning.

Unfortunately, several flaws in WEP have been uncovered as discussed in "WEP" in Chapter 1. Even with WEP turned on, a determined attacker can potentially log gigabytes worth of WEP-protected traffic in an effort to post-process the data and break the protection. These weaknesses in WEP drastically increase the risk due to eavesdropping. If WEP is cracked, there is great deal of sensitive data that is passed across networks with no further encryption, such as a user who accesses his mail using the POP or IMAP protocols. These protocols are widely deployed without any form of encryption for authentication or data transport, putting the users at risk when using a wireless network.

Manipulating

Manipulation takes eavesdropping a step further. An attacker who can successfully manipulate data on a network can effectively send data masquerading as a victim computer. Using ARP poisoning, an attacker can force traffic through a malicious machine. This malicious machine may, for example, change the content of emails, instant messages, or database transactions. The malicious machine can also choose not to forward packets along, effectively denying use of the network from the victim.

Illicit Use

Illicit use of a wireless network involves an attacker using the network because of its connection to other networks. Attackers may use a network to connect to the Internet or to connect to the corporate network that lives behind the AP. Illicit use may not cause any operational problems, but it still may be unwanted and unlawful use of the wireless network. An attacker in this case may simply be someone who drove up near the AP, associated to the network and is checking his mail. Alternatively, the attacker may be sending spam to thousands of email addresses. The attacker may even be attempting to exploit a file server that lives on the same network as the AP or use the AP as a mask to hide the source of illegal actions, such as hacking other networks.

No matter what the attacker is doing, his use is unacceptable. However, the different types of illicit use pose varying degrees of problems for the organization running the WLAN. Again, in a wired network, illicit use is not a likely problem. In order to use a wired network, an attacker must have physical access to the network infrastructure. For reasons already outlined, this is unlikely and generally risky for an attacker to do. However, in most wireless networks, an attacker has much more freedom and is less likely to be caught attempting to use the network. (Illicit use by authorized users is a different matter. They already have proper access to the network but are using it for activities that are forbidden by a network-usage policy.)

Access points are not difficult to find. An attacker can simply drive around an area looking for unprotected APs using war-driving software such as NetStumbler. Once an attacker finds an open AP, he can use it for whatever illicit use he desires.

Databases of APs have been created, removing the war-driving step. Some databases such as Cisco's Hotspot Locator (*http://www.cisco.com/pcgi-bin/cimo/Home*) provide the location of closed APs that require payment to access outside resources. Other databases such as The Shmoo Group's Global Access Wireless Database (*http://www.shmoo.com/gawd*) or NetStumbler's database (*http://www.netstumbler.com/query.php*) consist of APs entered by individuals who have encountered them via various means including war driving. An attacker can query any of these public databases to determine nearby APs to use as a launching point.

Illicit resource use is a risk for several reasons. An attacker may launch attacks against external servers. These attacks will be seen as originating from the IP addresses of the owner of the access point. If these exploits are detected by remote administrators, they will be tracked down to the owner of the AP. The AP owner may be subject to punishment from his ISP or even a criminal investigation. Without a clear and complete audit trail, this form of illicit use may cause large problems for the AP owner.

In addition, the AP owner may be paying for transit to the Internet on a usage basis. If an attacker is using relatively large amounts of bandwidth, his usage may cost the AP owner money. Even when Internet access is not paid for on a usage basis, the attacker may be using enough bandwidth to infringe on the legitimate use by other clients using the same Internet connection. If an attacker is downloading mp3s via a 265 kb/s DSL connection, then other users of the DSL connection may experience extremely slow connectivity to external services.

Wireless Risks

Many security professionals fall into the trap of dealing only with the theory and not the practice of defending a network. While it would be great to be protected from all potential attacks that a wireless network may come under, that level of protection may not be practical.

When securing your network, you must consider the risk associated with each attack and address it accordingly. The topic of risk assessment and risk management is one that could fill a book on its own. However, it is important that you understand the basics of risk assessment so you spend your time and money wisely addressing the real issues rather than waste resources on topics that present no risk.

Determining Risk

Figuring out your risk boils down to questions like: "What can happen?", "How likely is it to happen?", "What occurs when it happens?", and "How hard is it to defend against?". The "What can happen" question has already been answered in this chapter. Determining the likelihood of any particular attack is the next step.

The likelihood of an attack depends on factors such as:

How easy it is to launch the attack?
> An attack that is theoretical today may be widely distributed in "script kiddie" code tomorrow. The problems with WEP started out as a paper that described the theoretical problems with the protocol. Very few people had the ability to take the vulnerability and write code to exploit it. Within a few months, several

different exploit programs had been developed and were publicly available on the Internet. Once that code became available, the likelihood of WEP encrypted traffic being cracked became much higher

What is the risk to the attacker?

Home WLANs are great jumping-off points for hackers because home users tend not to be as diligent as larger corporations. An attacker may stay off large corporate WLANs for fear of being discovered by full-time security systems such as IDS systems and observant network engineers.

How big of a target are you and your assets?

A home network usually does not contain resources or people that will single out the network in the attentions of hackers. A bank network, on the other hand, may be filled with user IDs, passwords, high-profile executives, and (above all) money. Keep in mind that the prevalence of wide network scanning by hackers may make you a target simply because you are running a vulnerable service, not because of what valuable assets the network may contain.

There are other issues that affect likeliness, but this is the basic idea. When determining the likeliness of an attack, you must use some common sense and knowledge of the current state of the security industry.

Then you need to determine what you stand to lose (or gain) if a particular attack is used against your network. What kind of user IDs and passwords will be available on the network for eavesdroppers to pick up? Are there time-sensitive applications that a DoS attack can affect? Is the wireless network critical to the minute-to-minute operations of your organization? Can you afford to be sued if a hacker launches an attack from your network?

Finally, using the previous steps to prioritize your activities, you need to evaluate how difficult the attacks are to defend against. If protecting information on your network is your top priority, you must determine to what lengths you will go to protect the integrity of your data. If being sued due to illicit use is your biggest concern, then you must determine the steps you can reasonably take to detect illegitimate use.

When determining and prioritizing your risks, you do not need to necessarily go through a formal process. You need to evaluate your business requirements, your network, and your potential adversary. Most importantly, you need to think about practical ramifications as well as theoretical security.

Knowing Is Half the Battle

Now that you are familiar with the kinds of attacks that an attacker may commit, you know what you're protecting against. Once you've defined your risk in reference to these attacks, you need to know what tools are at your disposal to protect you and your users. The next step in setting up a secure wireless infrastructure is laying down a strong foundation in your wireless clients.

## PART II

Station Security

Wireless stations, the 802.11 terminology for client computers, are crucial to the security of the entire network. They often contain the most valuable resources, such as proprietary business documents or personal information and generate interesting network traffic, like email and online purchases. This data can be a target all in itself, but the client can also become an entry point into the network for an attacker. If an attacker can break into a client computer, he can use it as a means to access protected resources throughout the rest of the network. The chapters in this section will show you how to configure client stations securely on a wide range of platforms.

## CHAPTER 3

Station Security

Connecting to a wireless network puts your computer at risk. Eavesdroppers may intercept traffic sent between client stations and the access point. Malicious access points may attempt to force associations in order to perform man-in-the-middle attacks. Hackers using the same access point may try to exploit your computer. Due to the shared, physically unsecured nature of an 802.11 network, client stations are more likely to be the target of an attack.

Establishing proper security on stations connecting to a wireless network is the first step to creating a secure wireless infrastructure. The security of an entire infrastructure is like a chain; it is only as secure as its weakest link. Typically, wireless stations are laptops or workstations controlled by an individual, not by a team of security professionals. These stations may not be under the same scrutiny as a fileserver or firewall would be. Unfortunately, an unsecured wireless workstation can be an excellent vector for an attack on an entire infrastructure.

Client Security Goals

There are two main security considerations for safe usage of a client computer on a wireless network. The first is preventing a compromise of the client itself. A compromise of the client could lead to stolen or corrupted data, and provide an entry point for the attacker into the wider network. The second main consideration is using secure methods to communicate with other network services from the client.

Prevent Access to the Client

The client needs to be protected from attack over the network. The primary means of accomplishing this is through the use of a firewall. A firewall on a client should block all unknown incoming traffic and allow for outbound connections. Connections directly to or from other computers on the wireless network should also be blocked.

The exact means of accomplishing this for a specific OS will be covered in the five chapters that follow.

In addition to establishing a firewall, unneeded services on the client should be disabled. If there is a pressing reason to run a specific service from a client, firewall rules need to be modified to allow traffic to that service. It is vital that any exposed services are run using up-to-date software. Outdated software with security vulnerabilities is the primary entry point for attackers.

In addition, we'll discuss the use of static ARP to protect against layer 2 man-in-the-middle attacks. These attacks can lead to eavesdropping or manipulation of network sessions. The use of static ARP entries can prevent these attacks from succeeding, since the host will not modify its ARP table when it receives malicious information. Static ARP tables can be overwhelmingly complex to administer in large networks but can be a useful and easy tool in a smaller network. For more information on ARP attacks, see "ARP Poisoning" in Chapter 2.

Secure Communication

The manner in which you access services across the network is just as important as host security. It does not matter how bulletproof your firewall is if send your username and password in the clear every time you check your email with an IMAP request. Remember that an attacker can be passively listening to the network and not necessarily actively attacking your host.

At the time of this writing, WEP is not an acceptable solution for preserving the confidentiality of data traversing a wireless network. There are several problems with WEP that greatly weaken its effectiveness. WEP is better than *cleartext*; it raises the bar for an attacker to obtain transmitted data. However, a sophisticated attacker may still be able to bypass the encryption provided by WEP, thereby exposing your data.

In order to prevent sensitive data from being compromised, you need to provide for encryption at a higher level in the stack. Note that we did not say it was necessary to protect all of your data, just your sensitive data. Different users define sensitive information differently. While one user may think all data sent or received is sensitive, another may feel that there is no risk in an attacker seeing what web pages they are surfing. In general, you should work to protect usernames, passwords, credit-card information, and other unique, personal information. Whether or not you feel your DNS requests and Slashdot trolling are worthy of higher levels of encryption is up to you.

SSL

Secure Socket Layer (SSL) is a public-key, cryptography-based confidentiality mechanism. It is historically associated with web pages accessed via secure HTTP (HTTPS). However, any protocol can be encapsulated in SSL for secure network transit. SSL is great for protecting transaction-based protocols such as web traffic and mail transactions.

When surfing the Web using a wireless connection, you should pay special attention to pages that require you to authenticate yourself or that you have reached via authentication. Your initial authentication will involve sending your authentication credentials (i.e., username/password combinations) to the remote server. Unfortunately, subsequent pages accessed on the site after authentication may contain sensitive data, including your credentials or a cookie representing successful authentication. An attacker may be able to replay your authentication or your cookie to gain access to the same resources. Access to those pages and subsequent pages on the site should be accessed via HTTPS. The same advice goes for submission of credit-card information.

Web traffic is not the only candidate for SSL protection. Many mail clients allow for some form of SSL access to mail stores including Netscape's Messenger and the console-based mail reader *pine*. The most popular access mechanism is IMAP over SSL. When receiving mail via IMAP, your username and password must be sent to the remote mail server. Using SSL for this connection allows you to maintain the confidentiality of your mail access credentials. Some mail clients also support SMTP over SSL. However, since no authentication credentials are sent during an SMTP session, this practice is not as common. The use of SSL does increase the computational burden on the mail server and may not be feasible in high-volume mail systems. We value the privacy of our email and advise using SMTP or IMAP over SSL if available.

SSH

Secure Shell (SSH) is a secure replacement for the r-commands such as *rlogin*, *rcmd*, and *rshell*. SSH also uses public-key cryptography like SSL, but does not rely on a trusted authority to issue the public/private key pairs. SSH can use several symmetric ciphers when passing data between hosts to allow users to choose the appropriate level of security based on their situation. If it is not installed on your workstation, check your distribution media or *http://www.openssh.org* for links to the source code or precompiled binaries of OpenSSH.

When accessing a command shell on a remote machine over a wireless network, you should use SSH rather than telnet or the r-commands. When SSH is properly used, it will help ensure your credentials and traffic is protected from eavesdroppers.

SSH also provides a tunneling mechanism. A port on a local machine can be forwarded to a port on a remote machine. This allows secure access to remote services that are normally accessible in an insecure manner. This can be useful for accessing one particular service, but is not practical for tunneling many different types of traffic. The syntax for SSH local port forwarding is:

```
ssh -L localport:remotehost:remoteport username@remotehost
```

As an example, assume we are on a wireless network and want to access our IMAP server over SSH. Normally, IMAP credentials and email is sent in the clear. Due to the constant data stream involved in IMAP connections, they are ideal targets for eavesdroppers. By tunneling over SSH, the sensitive information is protected from malicious neighbors, as shown in Figure 3-1.

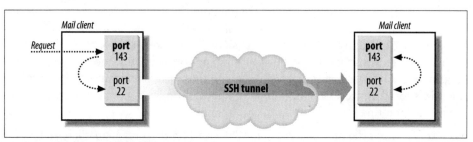

Figure 3-1. IMAP over SSH tunnel

In order to set up the tunnel, forward all local IMAP connections on the client (TCP port 143) to the IMAP port on the mail server. The following command performs the necessary remote port forwarding to achieve this:

```
ssh -f -L 143:mail.example.com:143 username@mail.example.com sleep 3600
```

In order to use this tunnel, configure your mail client to use localhost as the IMAP server. The −f flag tells SSH to go into the background after the authentication process is over. The command *sleep 3600* is executed on the remote host. Once the sleep command terminates, the SSH session will be torn down. This example can be modified to forward POP connections rather than IMAP by changing the port information to port 110.

Note that, by default, SSH will only forward connections that originate from localhost. Connections to forwarded ports from remote stations will be denied by default. In order to allow other machines to access the forwarded port, use the −g flag. Only do this if there is a reason for external connections.

Audit Logging

Even on client computers, it is very important to pay attention to the logs generated by the system. These logs can provide notification of attempted or successful compromises of system security. The location and format of these logs can vary from OS to OS. Monitoring of system logs can be tedious, and it is easy to become complacent. Because of this, we cover the installation of *swatch*, a basic tool to automate log monitoring.

Security Updates

After the system is set up, it is important to monitor the vendor web site for security patches. Most operating system vendors regularly discover or are notified of new security issues. Make it a habit to regularly check and download the latest patches, or use an automated updating system to gather them for you. When doing a fresh OS installation, it is a good idea to download any security patches on another machine and install them from a burned CD before connecting the fresh computer to the network.

## CHAPTER 4

FreeBSD Station Security

This chapter demonstrates how to lock down FreeBSD workstations for use on a wireless network. It will explain required and recommended kernel tuning, secure configuration of the wireless card, locking down the operating system, and adding third-party software to further enhance the security of the machine. Many of the security practices documented in this chapter are general best practices that should be applied to any workstation (but rarely are). However, without mechanisms geared for wireless security, standard wired network best practices alone are not enough.

FreeBSD Client Setup

FreeBSD has a long history of wireless networking support. FreeBSD had robust support for the original 802.11 cards and has continued to support 802.11b cards. As of this writing, several 802.11a cards have experimental support under FreeBSD-current. Unless otherwise noted, the examples given in this chapter are for FreeBSD 4.5-RELEASE. For information regarding this release or for questions on FreeBSD in general, please see *http://www.freebsd.org/*.

As in any other discussion of setting up a secure platform, the steps outlined below are governed by the *Principle of Least Privilege*. The Principle of Least Privilege means that a user or system should be given only the required amount of privilege to perform the required tasks. This principle can be extended to configuring an operating system. Only required services, kernel configuration options, users, and files should be installed. By having unneeded interfaces on a machine (such as ppp0) or leaving unnecessary services running, you provide an attacker potential vectors for compromising your machine.

Wireless Kernel Configuration

In order to use wireless NICs, the kernel must be configured to support the networking card. Complete instructions for compiling a kernel are outside the scope of this book. The information below is meant to supplement a normal kernel configuration. For information on compiling a new kernel, see */usr/share/doc/en/books/handbook/kernelconfig.html* on your FreeBSD system, or go to *http://www.freebsd.org/doc/en_US.ISO8859-1/books/handbook/kernelconfig.html*.

Before adding wireless and security options to your kernel, first remove all extraneous entries in your kernel configuration file. The GENERIC kernel that ships with FreeBSD contains many options that are not required for operation of most workstations. For example, if your workstation does not have any SCSI devices, remove all the SCSI devices and options from your kernel. Usually a configuration file for a workstation can be reduced to less than 100 lines. Once you have reached a minimal configuration, build a kernel and boot it. Verify that all devices are working as expected before adding the options specified in this section. The kernel parameters documented in this section are meant to supplement an existing kernel configuration file, not serve as a stand-alone kernel configuration.

In most cases, wireless NICs are connected via a PCMCIA (aka, PC-card) interface. For PCMCIA support, add the following to your kernel configuration file:

```
device        pcic0 at isa?
device        pcic1 at isa?
device        card
```

In order to get cards working after resuming a suspended laptop, you may also have to add this:

```
options       PCIC_RESUME_RESET
```

Once you have PC-card support, the kernel needs to be configured to use your wireless card. Card support is based on the internal chipset that the card runs on. Unfortunately, this information is not usually stamped on the outside of the card (or even in the documentation). In order to determine which chipset is in your card, you can search the Internet (including the vendor's web site) or simply compile all the drivers into the kernel. When the machine boots, you will be able to determine which driver is in use by the card. The other drivers can be removed from the kernel configuration at that point. The following list introduces the most common wireless interface driver types:

device awi
> This device is for legacy Prism I chipsets. Very few cards were sold using this chipset, so it is unlikely you will require this device.

device wi
> This device is for cards based on several chipsets including the Prism II chipset and Hermes chipset. Both of these are very common chipsets that have sold millions of units. Cards that use these chipsets include the D-Link DWL650, Orinoco Silver and Gold, and NetGear MA401.

device an

> This device is for Cisco Aironet cards. This includes both the Cisco 340 and 350 series cards.

device ray

> This device is for Raylink-based cards. The most common card based on this chipset is the Webgear Aviator.

You may also want to add the following options to your kernel:

```
options         WLCACHE
options         WLDEBUG
```

WLCACHE enables the wireless signal strength cache. The cache stores signal strength for every known MAC address on the network. Applications can then use the cache to determine the status of connections to other hosts. *WLDEBUG* allows for verbose wireless debugging. Low-level debugging can be useful when difficulty occurs while configuring a wireless card. Once enabled in the kernel, you can turn on debugging using *ifconfig <interface> debug*.

Security Kernel Configuration

After you get the wireless devices configured properly in the kernel, there is still more kernel tweaking to do. The FreeBSD kernel provides many security-specific options that help protect a machine and its users. These security parameters are the foundation for the host's security.

FreeBSD provides a kernel-level firewall that is controlled via the userland program *ipfw*. A firewall is critical piece to controlling the security of a wireless client. Your station and other stations associated to the same access point are in the same broadcast domain. There are no layer 3 or higher protection mechanisms between two stations in the same broadcast domain. A malicious user associated to the same access point as you has a "clear shot" at your machine. A host-based firewall running on your station can shut down IP-based attacks attackers may launch against you:

```
options         IPFIREWALL
```

This option enables the kernel-level firewall:

```
options         IPFIREWALL_VERBOSE
options         IPFIREWALL_VERBOSE_LIMIT=100
```

These options enable verbose logging for the firewall. This allows you to create a firewall ruleset that logs information about interesting packets to *syslog*. This logging leaves an audit trail that allows you to examine network activity on your machine. Setting a verbosity limit in the kernel keeps an attacker from filling up your filesystem with data about what packets are being dropped. Assume you have a firewall rule that denies and logs all inbound HTTP traffic (port 80). An attacker then sends millions of packets to port 80 on your machine. Without a logging limit, each one of these packets would be sent to *syslog* and written to disk. Eventually, the filesystem containing your log files would fill up, and your machine would, in all likelihood, crash:

options   IPFIREWALL_DEFAULT_TO_ACCEPT

Normally, the firewall denies all packets by default. This option allows you to accept packets by default. Allowing packets by default is a bad security practice. If the firewall rules are accidentally cleared or there is a mistake in your rules, a default policy of allowing traffic will leave you with an open system. This option should only be set if you have a pressing need to have the firewall "fail-open."

FreeBSD also allows for changing the default behavior of various network protocols. Most of these changes enhance the host's protection against denial-of-service attacks.

options   RANDOM_IP_ID

The *RANDOM_IP_ID* option changes the ID field in IP packets randomly rather than sequentially. This prevents third parties from guessing the rate at which the host is sending packets. It is also good practice when using link-level encryption such as WEP. Cryptoanalytic attacks can be launched against some ciphers when portions of the plaintext are known. By having a sequentially changing ID field, part of the plaintext is known by the attacker. While a small field like the IP ID may not be the key that allows a cryptographic protocol to be broken, it is still guessable data that will make a cryptographic attack a little bit easier.

options   TCP_DROP_SYNFIN

The TCP_DROP_SYNFIN causes the kernel to discard packets that have both the SYN and FIN bits set. Unless the hosts are utilizing the experimental TCP extensions outlined in RFC 1644, this should not cause any problems. Portscanning software such as *nmap* (available at *http://insecure.org*) will set both the SYN and FIN bits in an effort to avoid detection and determine what operating system the host is running. This option will make the OS determination more difficult.

options   ICMP_BANDLIM

This option limits the rate the host will respond to ICMP requests. This will help minimize the effects of denial-of-service attacks.

pseudo-device bpf

This is the Berkeley Packet Filter, which allows the root user to set a network interface into promiscuous mode. An interface in promiscuous mode will not only listen to frames destined for itself, but will pick up packets addressed for other hosts on the network. Normally, an interface will only process frames destined to that interface.

BPF is a double-edged sword. It can be a powerful troubleshooting tool for network and security problems. However, in the wrong hands, a BPF-enabled host is a liability to the security of a network. A malicious user can use a promiscuous mode interface to find user credentials and other sensitive data that is traversing a network. BPF is required for some monitoring tools, such as Arpwatch, which is discussed later in this chapter.

Startup Configuration

Several startup files need to be modified for your workstation to be fully functional at boot time. First, you must enable the PC-card services, which allows the system to use PCMCIA cards. (Some PCI wireless cards in desktop machines may not need to use PC card.) Then, the wireless network card needs to be configured for your particular wireless environment.

FreeBSD stores most of the startup directives in a file called */etc/ defaults/rc.conf*. In order to change a value specified in */etc/defaults/rc. conf* DO NOT edit that file directly. Put any line that needs to be changed into */etc/rc.conf*. At boot time, FreeBSD will override the defaults with values specified in */etc/rc.conf*.

Enable PC-card services by adding the following to */etc/rc.conf*:

```
pccard_enable="YES"
```

There are several ways to configure the wireless networking at startup. We prefer to have one file control all wireless networking activities. This allows a single point to manipulate all wireless parameters and generally simplifies administration of the machine. Create the following */usr/local/etc/rc.d/wireless.sh*:

```
#!/bin/sh
# This script will configure wireless network cards for FreeBSD
case "$1" in
start)

# Configure the Interface

    echo -n ' wireless network'
    ifconfig wi0 down
    ifconfig wi0 inet <your_ip_address> netmask <your_netmask> \
        ssid <your_ssid> wepmode <your_wepmode> wepkey \
        <your_wepkey> up
    # if you are going to use DHCP replace the above line with:
    # ifconfig wi0 ssid <your_ssid> wepmode <your_wepmode> wepkey \
    #     <your_wepkey<
    # dhclient wi0

# Set up default route

    route add default <your_default_gateway>

# Reset the firewall rules
```

```
    [ -x /etc/rc.firewall ] && sh /etc/rc.firewall && echo -n  \
        ' resetting firewall'
    ;;

stop)

# Take down the interface so no traffic can pass

    echo 'stopping wireless card'
    ifconfig wi0 down
    ;;
*)

# Standard usage statement

    echo "Usage: `basename $0` {start|stop}" >&2
    ;;
esac

exit 0
```

Make sure the file is executable by performing:

```
chmod 755 /usr/local/etc/rc.d/wireless.sh
```

At start time, this file will be executed during normal loading procedures with a *start* directive. If you need to reconfigure your card after boot time, you can execute this script by hand:

```
/usr/local/etc/rc.d/wireless.sh start
```

This script uses the command *ifconfig* to set both IP and wireless parameters. For more information on *ifconfig*, see the next section, "Card Configuration."

Card Configuration

The functionality of the wireless network card can be controlled by the *ifconfig* utility. Versions of FreeBSD prior to 4.5 used separate utilities to control wireless parameters. For Prism-based cards, configuration was performed via *wicontrol*. Cisco cards were controlled via *ancontrol*. The functionality of both utilities has been merged into *ifconfig* for the sake of consistency. As of 4.5, both *wicontrol* and *ancontrol* still exist for the sake of compatibility.

ifconfig usage includes the following parameters:

interface
> The name of the wireless interface to be managed.

*ssid **ssid***
> The Service Set Identifier of the preferred access point. By setting this value to ANY the station will associate to the access point with the strongest signal. This is not recommended, since a nearby attacker can cause your station to associate by providing a stronger signal.

*stationname **name***

> The name of the station the wireless card is installed in. This is not a required parameter.

*channel **number***

> The number of the channel the STA is to use. Under 802.11b networks governed by FCC regulations, this is a number between 1 and 11.

*authmode **mode***

> This is the mode the STA is to use when connecting to an infrastructure-based network. Values are none, open, and shared.

*wepmode **mode***

> This parameter indicates the method WEP will use for forming associations. off will allow the STA to be connected only to networks without WEP protection. on forces the STA to use WEP for associations. When set to on, the STA will not form an association unless the access point allows only WEP associations. mixed mode allows the STA to form non-WEP associations, but it will prefer WEP associations if they are available.

*weptxkey **index***

> The index is a value between 1–4 to indicate which WEP key is to be used for transmissions with the AP.

*wepkey key|**index:key***

> This specifies the value of the stored WEP keys. Four different keys can be stored by using index values between 1 and 4. The WEP key is specified as either an ASCII string or a hex value preceded by 0x.

There are other parameters that can be passed to *ifconfig*. They primarily deal with power-saving configuration to help extend the life of battery-operated devices.

For example, if you are connecting to the closed Example network using a WEP key of *secrt*, the following command would set up that association:

```
ifconfig wi0 ssid Example wepkey secrt wepmode on
```

ifconfig can also be used to query the state of the wireless NIC by passing the name of the interface as the only parameter. The previous example would result in the following:

```
bash-2.05# ifconfig wi0
wi0: flags=8843<UP,BROADCAST,RUNNING,SIMPLEX,MULTICAST> mtu 1500
        inet 192.168.0.100 netmask 0xffffff00 broadcast 192.168.0.255
        inet6 fe80::230:abff:fe0e:2e81%wi0 prefixlen 64 scopeid 0x6
        ether 00:30:ab:0e:2e:81
        media: IEEE 802.11 Wireless Ethernet autoselect (DS/11Mbps)
        status: associated
        ssid Example
        stationname "FreeBSD WaveLAN/IEEE node"
        channel 1 authmode NONE powersavemode OFF powersavesleep 100
        wepmode ON weptxkey 1
        wepkey 1:64-bit
```

OS Protection

A machine on a wireless network is in a hostile environment. With no physical security, any nearby host can launch an attack against a client with little or no protection offered by the network. Hosts must protect themselves via operating system configuration in order to be resilient to attack.

Firewall configuration

The first line of defense for hosts on a wireless network is a properly configured firewall. In general, most workstations will not be running any services, so configuring the firewall is relatively simple. Only outbound connections should be allowed in this case; all inbound connections should be dropped. If you do have services running on your workstation, you should configure your firewall appropriately.

The firewall configuration is stored in */etc/rc.firewall*. The file contains *ipfw* commands to configure the firewall based on parameters in */etc/rc.conf*. From the default FreeBSD *rc.firewall*:

```
#   open    - will allow anyone in
#   client  - will try to protect just this machine
#   simple  - will try to protect a whole network
#   closed  - totally disables IP services except via lo0 interface
#   UNKNOWN - disables the loading of firewall rules.
#   filename - will load the rules in the given filename (full path required)
```

For a workstation setup, your *rc.conf* should contain:

```
firewall_enable="YES"
firewall_type="CLIENT"
firewall_logging="YES"
```

Here is an example *rc.firewall* that should serve as a starting point for wireless clients. These commands should replace the commands in the "client" section of *rc.firewall*:

```
# Setup variables to allow for portable rulesets
net="<yoursubnet>"
mask="<yournetmask>"
ip="<youripaddress>"

# Allow active TCP sessions through.  The majority of the packets passed by
# the firewall will be handled by this rule, so it should be at the top of
# your ruleset.  Any active connections outbound from your workstation will
# be processed by this rule
${fwcmd} add pass tcp from any to any established

# Allow setup of outgoing TCP connections only
${fwcmd} add pass tcp from ${ip} to any setup

# Disallow and log setup of all other TCP connections
${fwcmd} add deny tcp from any to any setup log
```

```
# Allow DNS queries out in the world.  The "keep-state" parameter will cause
# the return DNS response to pass through the firewall.
${fwcmd} add pass udp from ${ip} to any 53 keep-state

# Silently drop local Windows queries.  They will quickly reach your log
# limit if you do not.
${fwcmd} add deny tcp from ${net}:${mask} to ${ip} 137-139
${fwcmd} add deny udp from ${net}:${mask} to ${ip} 137-139

# Log and deny connections from the local network.  There should never be
# any connections from the local network in a "hostile" wireless network.
${fwcmd} add deny ip from ${net}:${mask} to ${ip} log

# Log and deny everything else
${fwcmd} add deny ip from any to any log
```

You can examine the state of the firewall rulesets by executing the command *ipfw show*. The counters maintained by *ipfw* can be zeroed out by running *ipfw zero*.

The *ipfw* man page has information regarding further features that your firewall can utilize. Chapter 12 has a more complete discussion of creating gateway firewalls with FreeBSD to protect the wireless network.

Disable unneeded services

Unneeded services running on a host are one of the primary vectors for attackers to use to exploit machines. At the time of release for an operating system, there are generally no known security vulnerabilities in the default services. However, as time passes, security holes can be discovered in services and exploits can then be successfully written and executed against a vulnerable host.

If you are running services that are never actually used, you may very well forget that they exist. When a security vulnerability is found, you may not know to patch the service or you may simply not have time to patch the service before you are exploited. There is no need to run a service that provides no value and a large amount of risk.

In general, services are started in four places in FreeBSD: */etc/ined.conf*, */etc/rc.conf*, */etc/rc.d*, and */usr/local/etc/rc.d*. For services in */etc/rc.conf*, comment out the entry for the service that you don't want to start with a hash mark (#). Typically services started in *rc.conf* are *sshd* and *nfsd*. For services started out of *inetd.conf*, comment the service out with a hash mark (#). Services typically started out of *inetd.conf* are telnet and ftp. For services in the two *rc.d* directories, either remove the executable bit from the file or move the file to another directory. This is a matter of personal preference. Services started in these directories usually include *snmpd* and apache.

You can also use the setup and installation program */stand/sysinstall* to enable and disable services through a menu-driven system.

Static ARP

As documented in "ARP Poisoning" in Chapter 2, there is a real threat from man-in-the-middle attacks due to ARP poisoning. A malicious user may be able to convince your workstation that her host is the gateway by forging spoofed packets. By putting a static ARP entry on your host, the effectiveness of this attack is minimized.

Static ARP entries override any dynamic information received over the network. If you are always using the same gateway (i.e., you are not roaming around to different layer 3 wireless networks), you can put a script in */usr/local/etc/rc.d* to hardcode your gateway's ARP address. Create */usr/local/etc/rc.d/staticarp.sh* with the following information:

```
#!/bin/sh
# This script will set static arp entries for FreeBSD
case "$1" in
start)

# Add the MAC address for the gateway to the ARP table

    echo -n 'adding gateway MAC to arp table'
    arp -S <gatewayIP> <gatewayMAC>
    ;;

stop)

# Delete the MAC address from the ARP table

    echo 'removing static MAC from arp table'
    arp -d <gatewayIP>
    ;;
*)

# Standard usage statement

    echo "Usage: `basename $0` {start|stop}" >&2
    ;;
esac

exit 0
```

Make sure the file is executable by performing

```
chmod 755 /usr/local/etc/rc.d/staticarp.sh
```

Other security concerns

You can change other configuration settings, depending on your level of concern, but they are outside the scope of this book. It is up to you as an administrator and user to determine the level of risk you are willing to accept with your wireless workstations. For those looking to learn more about FreeBSD security, check out the security section of the FreeBSD handbook at *http://www.freebsd.org/doc/en_US.ISO8859-1/books/handbook/securing-freebsd.html*.

Audit Logging

Proper auditing of a host is critical to the ongoing security of a host. No matter how secure the initial setup of a machine is, the level of security decreases over time as new services are installed and new vulnerabilities are discovered.

arpwatch

As discussed in "ARP Poisoning" in Chapter 2, man-in-the-middle attacks can be launched via spoofing packets to a target host purporting to be from the gateway but with a malicious MAC address. This allows an attacker to intercept all traffic sent from your workstation.

In conjunction with setting a static ARP entry for the gateway (documented in "Static ARP"), other ARP entries can be monitored via the *arpwatch* utility. If you have the ports tree installed, you can perform the following to automatically install *arpwatch*:

```
cd /usr/ports/net/arpwatch
make
make install
```

If you do not have the ports tree installed, you can obtain *arpwatch* from *ftp://ftp.ee. lbl.gov/arpwatch.tar.gz* or use the command *pkg_add –r arpwatch* to have the system download the package and install it. Unpack the code and follow the instructions to build and install *arpwatch*. You need to have the Berkeley Packet Filter compiled into your kernel. See "Wireless Kernel Configuration" or "Security Kernel Configuration" earlier in this chapter for information on BPF support.

Once *arpwatch* is installed, you can configure it to mail a user whenever an event is detected. On a normal network, there are very few ARP events of interest so there will be few emails sent. When there is an ARP-based attack under way, *arpwatch* can generate quite a large quantity of email. By adding *-m <youremailaddress>* to the *arpwatch* commands in */usr/local/etc/rc.d/arpwatch.sh*, these events will be mailed to a user of your choosing. Ideally this email will be sent to a local account so it will not swamp remote mail servers in the event of a large attack and can be monitored in near real time.

If *arpwatch* reports a flip-flop, it means an IP address has been hijacked for an existing host on the network. This may be due to simple misconfiguration, where a user has inadvertently duplicated another IP address on the network. It may also be an attacker attempting to either hijack an active session or perform a man-in-the-middle attack. Here is an example of a flip-flop:

```
From: arpwatch (Arpwatch)
To: root@localhost
Subject: flip flop
Status: 0

         hostname: <unknown>
```

```
          ip address: 192.168.0.1
    ethernet address: 0:2:2d:8:5b:30
     ethernet vendor: Agere Systems
old ethernet address: 0:30:ab:e:2e:81
 old ethernet vendor: DELTA NETWORKS, INC.
           timestamp: Thursday, February 14, 2002 2:46:21 +0000
  previous timestamp: Thursday, February 14, 2002 2:45:49 +0000
               delta: 32 seconds
```

The old Ethernet address is from a wired Ethernet vendor. This was the Ethernet card on the network's gateway (192.168.0.1). The new Ethernet address is from Agere Systems, a large vendor of wireless networking equipment. This is an attacker on the wireless network attempting to poison the ARP cache of other hosts on the network to perform a man-in-the-middle attack. After receiving this email, you need to make a decision about the integrity of the network you are attached to. If you feel the network is untrustworthy, then you should disconnect from the network and notify the network administrator.

syslog

The *syslog* facility is the central log collector for any UNIX host, and FreeBSD is no exception. The log files controlled by *syslog* can provide a wealth of information. Some attacks that will be performed against wireless clients are known and are easy to find in a log. Over time, new attacks will be launched which will not match any known signature. With a complete-enough audit trail, you may be able to reconstruct events in an unknown attack. Once the reconstruction is complete you can then determine the best mechanism to use to defend yourself from the attack.

In order to review the information, the log data needs to be redirected to the proper log files. Rather than break apart the log data into different files based on log facility and severity, it is sometimes useful to send all log data to one file. This allows the data to be distilled using tools such as *grep* and *perl*. These unique views of audit data tend to be much more useful than splitting the data up a priori.

In order to log all data sent to *syslog* to */var/log/messages*, add the following line to the top of your */etc/syslog.conf*:

```
    *.*                         /var/log/messages
```

Be sure to comment out any other line that references */var/log/message* in the *syslog* configuration file with a hash mark (#). To force these changes to take effect without rebooting, execute *killall syslogd; syslogd* as root.

swatch

swatch is a utility to monitor log files and report on interesting strings. It serves as a set of eyes constantly watching your log files. Upon finding a pre-specified string in a log file, swatch can send email, ring the bell, or execute arbitrary system commands.

It is incredibly flexible and can be a lifesaver for those of us who do not like watching log files out of the corner of our eyes.

If you have the ports tree installed, you can execute the following commands to install *swatch*:

```
cd /usr/ports/security/swatch
make
make install
```

If you do not have the ports tree installed, you can get the source code for *swatch* at *http://www.oit.ucsb.edu/~eta/swatch/*. Install the source according to the instructions included in the source code.

Once installed, you need to determine what strings you want to look for and what actions you want to take when you find them. Ideally you want to monitor connection attempts from other hosts on the wireless network. This is an indication of some potentially malicious activity. The following is an example of a *swatch* configuration file that will ring a bell for every log entry created due to a request from a local machine. The local subnet in this example is 192.168.0.0:255.255.255.0:

```
# swatchrc.personal example to watch for connection attempts from
# local machines

watchfor    /Deny TCP 192.168.0/
        echo
        bell
```

swatch is quite customizable. After getting familiar with normal and abnormal log traffic on your host, expand this *swatch* configuration file to suit your needs.

Now that your FreeBSD client is secure, you have a fighting chance of maintaining the integrity of your workstation while using a wireless network. By securing the operating system and supporting programs, you make it difficult for an attacker to subvert your host. Layering proper auditing features on top of the strong layer of security helps you watch for the unknown. When new attacks are launched, hopefully you will have enough information to unwderstand what is happening to your host and react accordingly.

## CHAPTER 5

Linux Station Security

Computers on a wireless network are at risk of attack from anyone nearby. Since there are not the same physical bounds to network access that there are in a wired network, clients are at a much higher risk of attacks. Linux is a powerful, complex operating system. Properly configured, a Linux host can withstand sustained attacks from dedicated attackers. Unfortunately, a poorly configured Linux machine can be a dangerous weapon for an attacker and a liability to you as an individual.

Linux Client Setup

Wireless support in Linux has progressed dramatically over the past several years. FreeBSD used to be the operating system of choice for WLAN usage, but the support now available under Linux makes it a great operating system for wireless networking. Linux supports many common 802.11b cards. Many vendors developing 802.11a and 802.11g equipment are developing Linux drivers at the same time as their Windows drivers. Other vendors are deploying embedded Linux systems with wireless support.

Unless otherwise noted, the examples given in this chapter are performed on RedHat Linux 7.2 with kernel 2.4.18. The examples should work on most recent Linux distributions, but may require small changes to the scripts or file locations. For more information regarding RedHat Linux, see *http://www.redhat.com*. For more information on kernel 2.4.18, see *http://www.kernel.org*.

Kernel Configuration

In order to securely use a wireless network, you must start with a secure host configuration. At the heart of any secure host is a solid, well-planned kernel configuration. A secure kernel must be governed by the Principle of Least Privilege. The Principle of Least Privilege indicates that a user or system should only be given the minimum amount of privilege in order to achieve the desired tasks. This means that a kernel should be stripped of all unneeded configuration options. If you don't have any SCSI devices, then you shouldn't have any SCSI devices specified in your kernel configuration.

Wireless Kernel Configuration

In order to use wireless NICs, the kernel must be configured to support the networking card. The process of compiling a Linux kernel is outside the scope of this book. For more information on compiling a kernel, see */usr/src/linux-2.4/README* on your Linux system or *http://www.tldp.org/HOWTO/Kernel-HOWTO.html.* Configure and compile a kernel with as few configurations options as possible. Once you have a bare-bones kernel for your machine, continue with the steps in the rest of this chapter.

There are many ways to configure a kernel. Whether you use *make menuconfig, make xconfig,* or simply *make config*, the changes are saved to a configuration file. This file is typically in */usr/src/linux-2.4/configs/kernel-[ver].config.* The configuration options specified in this chapter are directives in that file. How they get written to the file is up to you; you can edit it directly, or use the make *_config scripts.

Wireless NICs are generally connected to either an internal PCI connector or a PCM-CIA (PC-card) interface. You must first enable whichever interface type you are going to be using. PCI support, probably already compiled in your kernel, is enabled with the following:

```
CONFIG_PCI=y
```

There is support in the Linux kernel for various PCI-based wireless cards including those made by Lucent, Cisco, and Linksys. Consult the kernel documentation to determine how to add support for your particular card.

PCMCIA can be added several ways. The easiest way to get wireless PC-card support on a 2.4 kernel is via the *pcmcia-cs* package, which is available from *http://pcmcia-cs.sourceforge.net/.* In order to use *pcmcia-cs*, you must enable loadable modules and disable native PC-card support:

```
CONFIG_MODULES=y
CONFIG_CARDBUS=y
```

Next, enable wireless networking support. This is also known as "non-hamradio" support:

```
CONFIG_NET_RADIO=y
```

You should be able to make and install your kernel at this point. Everything else is handled via the *pcmcia-cs* package.

Most Linux distributions ship with precompiled *pcmcia-cs* modules. You can probably use the precompiled distribution of *pcmcia-cs* with no problems. If you have a reason to compile *pcmcia-cs* by hand (or are feeling adventurous), then press on.

Download the *pcmcia-cs* source from *http://pcmcia-cs.sourceforge.net/*. Uncompress the source code in the same directory that contains the root of your Linux source code (usually */usr/src*). Enter the directory that was created during the decompression and run *make config*. You will be asked the following questions:

Alternate target install directory?
> You can specify where your Linux source code is. This defaults to */usr/src/linux*.

Build "trusting" versions of card utilities?
> Normally, the utilities created in this package must be run by root to make changes to the card configuration. A "trusting" utility allows any user to modify the configuration of the card. Only build a trusting utility if you are sure this is what you want.

Include 32-bit (CardBus) card support?
> If you have CardBus cards you want to use, you must enable this feature. Even if you do not have CardBus cards at this point, it is usually safe to enable this feature.

Include PnP BIOS resource checking?
> PnP BIOS resource checking allows *pcmcia-cs* to try to avoid resource conflicts on the host. However, this option may cause problems on some machines. You may or may not have to use this option.

Module install directory?
> You can specify an alternate module directory if needed.

Once you have answered these questions, run *make all* then *make install*. Review the files in */etc/pcmcia* to see if any changes need to be made to accommodate your equipment. Reboot the machine to verify your card is now recognized by the host.

Security Kernel Configuration

Now that the wireless devices are working properly, it is time to add security enhancements to the kernel. These security options will provide you with a hardened core for the rest of your client to use.

A firewall provides a primary line of defense against attacks from the network. This is particularly important in wireless networks. Two clients on the same access point typically have no network-level access control mechanism preventing them from communicating. Therefore, it is up to the client to defend itself from attacks from malicious wireless users.

Linux provides a robust firewalling mechanism called Netfilter. The Netfilter firewall is implemented in the kernel and controlled by a userland program called *iptables*. Previous versions (Version 2.2 and earlier) of Linux used a firewall called IPFW that could be controlled by either *ipfwadm* or *ipchains*, but these mechanisms have been deprecated. This chapter concentrates solely on using Netfilter and *iptables* to protect a client. For a more complex usage of Netfilter, see Chapter 11, where a Linux gateway configuration is explored.

Enable Netfilter with the following option:

```
CONFIG_NETFILTER=y
```

There are many configuration options for Netfilter. Some are required, however most of the following options can be added at your discretion based on your needs:

CONFIG_IP_NF_IPTABLES
> This option provides the framework in the kernel that *iptables* uses to manage the firewall. This option is required.

CONFIG_IP_NF_FILTER
> This option allows the firewall to filter packets that the host is attempting to send and receive. This option is required.

CONFIG_IP_NF_MATCH_MAC
> This option allows the firewall to match packets based on source and destination MAC addresses. This can be very useful on a wireless network where IP spoofing is very easy to perform.

CONFIG_IP_NF_MATCH_STATE
> This parameter turns Netfilter into a stateful firewall. Stateful firewalls are able to keep track of active and legitimate sessions. After a packet has been sent and received forming a two-way conversation, the firewall will add that session to a state table. This state table allows for faster parsing of packets in an established session as well as preventing forged established packets from getting through (this is a problem with packet filtering firewalls such as IPFW). This option is not required but is very strongly recommended, as our examples make use of these features.

CONFIG_IP_NF_CONNTRACK
> This option allows connections to be tracked by the firewall. This makes use of the stateful nature of Netfilter to track established connections in a more efficient manner.

CONFIG_IP_NF_FTP
> This module adds logic for tracking FTP connections in the firewall. FTP connections are historically difficult for firewalls to handle since they have separate command and data channels. With this module, both active and passive mode FTP are possible.

CONFIG_IP_NF_IRC
> This is similar to the FTP connection-tracking module. It provides higher-level logic to allow the firewall to properly track IRC connections.

CONFIG_IP_NF_TARGET_LOG

This option allows the firewall to log packets to syslog for further examination. Logging a packet sends a great deal of information regarding the packet to the log facility allowing for very detailed analysis of an ongoing attack.

This should be enough to configure a robust client firewall. For an example of a client Netfilter configuration, see "Firewall Configuration" in this chapter.

CONFIG_SYN_COOKIES

This option allows for a SYN-flood mitigation technique called SYN Cookies to be used. SYN Cookies work by creating a cryptographic challenge in the ACK packet to verify a SYN packet is part of a legitimate session. It takes up a fair bit of resources on the host when turned on. Even when allowed in the kernel, SYN Cookies are turned off by default. You can enable them by issuing the following command:

```
echo 1 >/proc/sys/net/ipv4/tcp_syncookies
```

This should not be required on a machine that is only a workstation and not a server. If you are running any services on your machine you should at least have SYN Cookies support enabled.

CONFIG_PACKET=y

This configuration options allows raw packets to be captured from an interface. This is similar to BPF support in the FreeBSD kernel. A root user can use the packet capability to listen for frames destined for other machines on the network. This option is required to run programs such as *tcpdump* or *arpwatch*.

Startup Configuration

At boot time, the wireless NIC needs to be initialized with the proper information. All wireless specific information is stored in */etc/pcmcia/wireless.opts*. The file that comes with your distribution probably has entries for different cards. While having the ability to select different network settings for different cards may be useful, it is not normal. Most people will want to have the same network setting regardless of what card they are using. You can accomplish this using the following as a template:

```
case "$ADDRESS" in
*,*,*,*)
    # INFO - name describing this connection
    INFO="Wireless Netork"
    # ESSID - Name of ESSID to join.
    ESSID="Example"
    # MODE - Operation Mode.  Common values are Managed for associations
    # to an access poing and Ad-Hoc to join an iBSS
    MODE="Managed"
    # RATE - Data rate of the connection.  Auto allows the card to
    # select the best for the condition.
    RATE="auto"
    # KEY - WEP key.  Hex keys are entered like 0123-4567-89.  ASCII
```

```
                # keys are pre-pended with an s.  s:secrt
                KEY="s:secrt"
                ;;
        esac
```

The default *wireless.opts* file has more values that can be configured based on your needs. Read through the file if you require a more advanced configuration. All of the values set in *wireless.opts* are passed to *iwconfig* to configure the card. For information on *iwconfig*, see the next section, "Card Configuration."

The default startup files should handle getting the interface up and configured beyond the wireless options. However, the interface will probably be configured for DHCP by default. If you wish to configure a static IP address, you will have to edit */etc/sysconfig/network-scripts/ifcfg-[device]*. This is an example of an ifcfg-eth0 set to a static IP address:

```
        DEVICE=eth0
        IPADDR=192.168.0.100
        NETMASK=255.255.255.0
        NETWORK=192.168.0.0
        BROADCAST=192.168.0.255
        GATEWAY=192.168.0.1
        ONBOOT=yes
```

For a client that will use DHCP to acquire an address, the following can be used instead:

```
        DEVICE=eth0
        ONBOOT=yes
        BOOTPROTO=DHCP
```

Card Configuration

Configuring a wireless NIC under Linux is a two-step process. The wireless-specific parameters must be set using the *iwconfig* utility. Once the card has formed a proper association with an access point, then the IP specific information should be configured via the *ifconfig* utility.

iwconfig uses the following configuration parameters:

interface
>   This is the name of the interface to be configured. Typically this value will be something like eth0. If *iwconfig* is passed the interface name only and no other configuration parameters, it will return the current configuration of the wireless interface.

essid essid
>   This is the name of the Extended Service Set ID (ESSID) to join. This value must the same as the similar value on the access point. A value of any will cause the client to associate with the strongest detected access point. This is not recom-

mended since a nearby attacker may force your client to reassociate with a hostile access point.

nwid nwid

This is the network ID. A network ID is a mechanism used to identify particular access points within an SSID. Many access points may have the same SSID and therefore provide service to the same network. However the *nwid* for each access point may be different, allowing users to "hard code" what access point they wish to associate with. A value of off will disable *nwid* checking. This value is not required.

channel channel

This is the channel used to communicate with the access point. The 802.11b PHY specification describes channels in the 2.4 GHz ISM band for use by 802.11b radios. In the U.S., there are 11 usable channels, while European countries have 14. The client must specify the same channel as the access point in order to be able to communicate with it.

mode mode

This is the type of network in which the client will participate. The options are managed for associations with access points and ad-hoc for forming associations in IBSS mode.

ap mac-addr

This is the MAC address of the requested access point. By setting this parameter, the client will only associate with an access point with the specified MAC address. This is useful to minimize the risk presented by nearby rogue access points attempting to spoof your SSID and NWID. An example of this flag is ap 00:08:20:4e:5e:1f. This flag is not required.

key [wepkey] [index] [mode]

This flag controls all the WEP configuration options. The WEP key may be entered as hex (e.g., 0123-4567-89) or ASCII pre-pended with s: (e.g., s:secrt). Multiple keys can be entered and referenced by specifying an index value between 0 and 3. Finally, the association mode can be set to control how the client handles WEP and non-WEP packets. on and off turn WEP protection on and off, respectively. open allows the card to form WEP or non-WEP associations based on what access points are available. restricted will force the card to form WEP-only associations.

This is not a complete list of the flags that can be passed to *iwconfig*. Other options include power-saving configurations, sensitivity requirements, and client-side identification issues. For a complete list of supported flags, run *man iwconfig*.

For example, if you are connecting to the closed Example network using a WEP key of *secrt*, the following command would setup that association:

```
iwconfig eth0 essid Example key s:secrt restricted
```

iwconfig can also be used to query the state of the wireless NIC by passing only the interface name as a parameter:

```
[root@mo root]# iwconfig eth0

eth0      IEEE 802.11-DS  ESSID:"Example"  Nickname:"Prism  I"
          Mode:Managed  Frequency:2.412GHz  Access Point: 00:02:2D:04:3D:5D
          Bit Rate:2Mb/s   Tx-Power=15 dBm   Sensitivity:1/3
          RTS thr:off   Fragment thr:off
          Encryption key:3433-6435-64
          Power Management:off
          Link Quality:92/92  Signal level:-11 dBm  Noise level:-102 dBm
          Rx invalid nwid:0  invalid crypt:0  invalid misc:0
```

The WEP key is displayed by *iwconfig* because the command was run as root. If a non-root user runs *iwconfig*, the encryption key will not be in the output.

Once the wireless-specific information has been configured, any IP information can be configured as usual with *ifconfig*. While FreeBSD allows you to configure all wireless and IP parameters via the *ifconfig* utility, Linux requires two different programs to be run in order to achieve the same result.

Card Utilities

There are several other *iw*-based commands that can be useful for configuring a client card:

iwgetid interface
> This command will return the value of the SSID of the access point to which the client is currently associated.

iwlist [interface] [freq | ap | rate | key | power | txpower | retry]
> This command will return various statistics from the wireless interfaces on the client computer and is useful for determining the capabilities of the card. For example, `iwlist key` will list the available key lengths and the existing keys stored on the card. `iwlist rate` will give the various data rates at which the card is capable of transmitting.

iwspy interface {+] IPADDR | HWADDR [...]
> Iwspy is a mechanism to track the quality of a link between your node and another on the wireless network. You must first set what IP or MAC address you wish to track (e.g., `iwspy 192.168.0.1`). Pre-pending a + to the list of addresses will add the address set to the end of the existing set of addresses being tracked. Once you are tracking addresses, you can then check the status of that link by passing only the name of the interface:

```
[root@mo root]# iwspy eth0
eth0      Statistics collected:
    00:60:1D:20:E0:00 : Quality:91/92  Signal level:-11 dBm  Noise level:-102 dBm
(updated)
```

```
iwpriv interface private-command [private-parameters]
```
This command can set driver-specific parameters which are not accessible via the *iwconfig* command set. For instance, if you need to enable the roaming features which exist in the wavelan_cs drivers, you would use *iwpriv* to do so.

Finally, you can query the status of any wireless interface via the */proc* filesystem:

```
[root@mo root]# cat /proc/net/wireless
Inter-| sta-|   Quality        |   Discarded packets              |\
Missed
 face | tus | link level noise |   nwid  crypt    frag  retry   misc|\ beacon
  eth0: 0000   92.  245.  154.        0       0       0       0       0 \       0
```

OS Protection

A secure kernel is only part of the solution for using a wireless network securely. A station on a wireless network is in a hostile environment. Anyone nearby can launch an attack against the station. The station should not rely on other network defenses to keep these attacks at bay; it must defend itself from hostile activity.

Firewall Configuration

The firewall configuration on a wireless client is relatively simple. Most clients are not running any services such as web or mail servers. The only new connections should be outbound from the host; there should be no inbound connection requests. If you do have services running on your client, you will need to modify your firewall configuration appropriately.

The Netfilter firewall included in Linux 2.4 is controlled by the program *iptables*. In a nutshell, Netfilter uses a list of firewall rules called *chains* to process packets. There are three different chains in a Netfilter firewall:

INPUT
> Packets destined for the host machine are handled by the INPUT chain. If a host is running a web server, packets destined for port 80 on the host's public IP address would be handled by the INPUT chain.

OUTPUT
> The OUTPUT chain processes packets generated by the host for another host. A request by your workstation for a web page from a remote web server would be handled by your workstation's output chain.

FORWARD
> The FORWARD chain processes packets that are sourced by a non-local host and destined for a non-local host. This type of action is typical of a firewall protecting an entire network where traffic is moving through the host, not actually destined for the firewall itself.

In order to manage the firewall, you need to create a shell script that invokes the proper *iptables* commands to implement your desired ruleset. The example file below is a simple firewall configuration for a wireless client. It makes use of the stateful options in Netfilter. Be sure to have the appropriate modules compiled into the firewall as documented in "Security Kernel Configuration" earlier in this chapter. For more information on *iptables* and Netfilter, see Chapter 11, *http://www.netfilter.org/*, or the *iptables* man page.

```
#!/bin/sh
# simple rc.firewall to for wireless client

# setup variables
IPTABLES=/sbin/iptables

# flush all chains to get a clean start
$IPTABLES -flush

# Both INPUT and FORWARD chains will be jumped to the user-defined
# "client" chain
# Create the client chain
$IPTABLES -N client

# Allow any established traffic through
$IPTABLES -A client -m state --state ESTABLISHED,RELATED -j ACCEPT

# Accept any new connections that are not coming in the primary Ethernet
# interface (the wireless interface)
$IPTABLES -A client -m state -state NEW -i ! eth0 -j ACCEPT

# Drop everything else
$IPTABLES -A client -j DROP

# Jump the INPUT and FORWARD chains to the client chain
$IPTABLES -A INPUT -j client
$IPTABLES -A FORWARD -j client

# allow all outbound traffic
$IPTABLES -A OUTPUT -j ACCEPT
```

Save this as an executable file at */etc/init.d/rc.firewall*. Then add the following lines to */etc/rc.d/rc.local*:

```
# IP Firewall
echo "starting IP Firewall"
/etc/init.d/rc.firewall
```

At the next reboot, your firewall rules will take effect. To immediately apply the firewall rules, run */etc/init.d/rc.firewall*. Some distributions may have an alternate way to load firewall rules at boot time. Refer to your distribution's documentation for any potential issues.

Disable Unneeded Services

The Principle of Least Privilege not only applies to kernel compiling but also to services running on your workstation. Extraneous services running on your host are potential vectors for attackers to compromise your machine. The more services you have running, the higher the likelihood of one of them having a security vulnerability. Determine what services you need to have running and disable all others. By disabling unneeded services, you minimize your exposure to the attack and simplify your job as a systems administrator.

You can determine what services you are offering by using the –i flag with the *lsof* utility:

```
[root@mo etc]# lsof -i
COMMAND    PID USER   FD   TYPE DEVICE SIZE NODE NAME
portmap    639 root    3u  IPv4    913      UDP *:sunrpc
portmap    639 root    4u  IPv4    914      TCP *:sunrpc (LISTEN)
rpc.statd  668 root    4u  IPv4    939      UDP *:844
rpc.statd  668 root    5u  IPv4    966      UDP *:1024
rpc.statd  668 root    6u  IPv4    969      TCP *:1024 (LISTEN)
sshd       933 root    3u  IPv4   1198      TCP *:ssh (LISTEN)
xinetd     966 root    3u  IPv4   1222      TCP mo:1025 (LISTEN)
xinetd     966 root    3u  IPv4   1273      TCP *:echo
sendmail  1006 root    4u  IPv4   1274      TCP mo:smtp (LISTEN)
X         1233 root    1u  IPv4   1477      TCP *:x11 (LISTEN)
```

The commands on the left have opened the ports specified on the right. On this host, echo and sendmail (*smtp*) are running. These services are probably not necessary and can be shut off. According to *lsof*, the echo port is controlled by *xinetd*, while the sendmail port is controlled by sendmail itself. In order to disable these services I will have to find the sendmail configuration and disable it and modify the *xinetd* configuration to stop launching echo.

Services can be started in any number of ways on a Linux machine. Many services, such as telnet, ftp, and portmapper are launched by a super daemon such as *inetd* or *xinetd*. *inetd* has been the standard super daemon for quite a while. However, some distributions such as RedHat have migrated to *xinetd* due to its enhanced feature set and security.

Services started through *inetd* are controlled via *inetd.conf* (usually found in */etc*). You can stop services launched by *inetd* by commenting them out of *inetd.conf* with a hash mark (#). These changes will take effect on the next reboot. To have the changes take effect immediately, send a HUP signal to *inetd* to force it to reread its configuration file:

```
killall -s HUP inetd
```

xinetd configuration is a bit different. On most systems, there is a configuration wrapper file at */etc/xinetd.conf*. This file calls scripts located in */etc/xinetd.d/*. To disable services listed in *xinetd.d*, add the following line to the configuration file for the desired service:

```
disable = yes
```

Again, changes will take effect on the next reboot. *xinetd* will not reread its configuration file when sent a HUP signal. The process must be terminated completely and restarted for changes to take effect immediately:

```
killall xinetd; xinetd -stayalive -reuse -pidfile \
    /var/run/xinetd.pid
```

For a tutorial on all that xinetd has to offer, see *http://www.macsecurity.org/resources/xinetd/tutorial.shtml*.

For services not launched out of a super daemon, they are probably launched out of one of the runlevel startup directories. The startup files are stored in varied locations depending on your distribution, for example, */etc/rc.d/rc[0-6].d* on RedHat and */etc/rc[0-6].d* on Debian. The number corresponds to the runlevel in which the scripts are invoked. Most of the time, the scripts you will want to disable are in rc2.d and rc3.d. To disable a service in the *rc* directories, rename the file to start with something other than an S, usually a K. For example, in order to disable sendmail on RedHat, perform the following:

```
cd /etc/rc.d/rc2.d
mv S80sendmail K80sendmail
```

Sendmail will not start at the next reboot.

Static ARP

ARP poisoning attacks, discussed in Chapter 2, are a real threat to all entities on a wireless network. A host on a wireless network can fall victim to a man-in-the-middle or DoS attack due to a malicious user poisoning your ARP cache. By statically assigning MAC-to-IP address mapping for important hosts on the network, you can minimize the risk posed by ARP poisoning attacks.

At the very least, you should set a static ARP entry for your default gateway. The following is an example file which you can place in */etc/init.d/staticarp* to perform that task. Replace the <gatewayIP> and <gatewayMAC> with your specific values:

```
#!/bin/sh
# This script will set static arp entries for Linux
case "$1" in
start)

# Add the MAC address for the gateway to the ARP table

    echo -n 'adding gateway MAC to arp table'
    arp -s <gatewayIP> <gatewayMAC>
    ;;
```

```
    stop)

    # Delete the MAC address from the ARP table

        echo 'removing static MAC from arp table'
        arp -d <gatewayIP>
        ;;
    *)

    # Standard usage statement

        echo "Usage: `basename $0` {start|stop}" >&2
        ;;
    esac

    exit 0
```

In order to have the ARP entries loaded automatically at boot time, make sure the file is executable and add a symlink in */etc/rc.d/rc2.d*:

```
[root@mo rc2.d]# chmod 755 /etc/init.d/staticarp
[root@mo rc2.d]# cd /etc/rc.d/rc2.d
[root@mo rc2.d]# ln -s /etc/init.d/staticarp S98staticarp
```

Other Security Concerns

Depending on your level of paranoia, you can further secure your workstation. These enhanced security concerns are outside the scope of this book. A good reference on Linux security is the Linux Security HOWTO available at *http://www.tldp.org/ HOWTO/Security-HOWTO.html*.

Audit Logging

No matter how strong your security mechanisms are, if you are not logging and monitoring your logs, you are vulnerable to unforeseen attacks. Diligent logging and monitoring gives you the ability to react to attacks in real time, protecting yourself and your resources.

arpwatch

Due to the lack of physical security in a wireless network, low-level attacks are of a much greater concern than they would be on a wired network. ARP poisoning, as discussed in Chapter 2, allows a malicious host to act as a man in the middle for machines on the network. The static ARP settings discussed earlier in this chapter are one way to protect yourself from ARP-based problems.

However, being able to detect ARP issues on the network gives you a window into the overall security of the network. If someone on the network is attempting ARP spoofing attacks, it is safe to assume your packets are being sniffed and your data is a risk. A program called *arpwatch* will watch the network for you and report any unusual activity. In order to use *arpwatch*, the program must have access to raw frames being sent across the wire. This requires CONFIG_PACKET support in your kernel.

For a complete discussion of *arpwatch* and how to configure it, see "arpwatch" in Chapter 4.

syslog

syslog is a common audit facility that any application on a host can use. Many standard applications as well as the kernel log send very useful information to *syslog*. Being able to direct *syslog* data to a desired location and monitor it gives you a view into what your system is doing as well as what others are trying to do to it.

Different Linux distributions have different *syslog* configurations. In general, they are configured to send *syslog* to many different logfiles based on *syslog* facility and severity. Rather than break apart the log data into different files, it is sometimes useful to send all log data to one file. This allows the data to be distilled using tools such as *grep* and *perl*. These unique views of audit data tend to be much more useful than splitting the data up a priori.

In order to log all data sent to *syslog* to */var/log/messages*, add the following line to the top of your */etc/syslog.conf*:

```
    *.*                           /var/log/messages
```

Be sure to comment out any other line that references */var/log/messages* in the *syslog* configuration file with a hash mark (#). To force these changes to take effect without rebooting, execute *killall syslogd; syslogd* as root.

swatch

Watching logfiles is boring. When there are no interesting events in a logfile, it is easy to lose interest and stop paying attention. It is also impossible to watch logfiles all the time. *swatch* is a program designed to watch logfiles for you. It will *tail* (continuously monitor what is being written to) any ASCII logfile and watch it for interesting strings. *swatch* can be configured to alert you via email, console messages, or even a system beep when it detects a problem. For a complete discussion of *swatch*, see "swatch" in Chapter 4.

Secure Communication

No matter how strong your firewall is, and no matter how solid your kernel configuration is, if you send your mail password in the clear across the network, you have subverted all the security built into your system. Secure communication is the keystone in client-side security. For a full discussion of secure communication mechanisms, see "Secure Communication" in Chapter 3.

With your FreeBSD and Linux wireless clients secured, you can compensate for a hostile and insecure network. By locking down your workstation, an attacker will likely get frustrated attempting to attack your machine and will move on to another host on the network. The next steps in secure wireless networking are to examine the security of the access point and the network gateway.

CHAPTER 6

OpenBSD Station Security

OpenBSD has focused on providing a free, functional, and secure operating system. The OpenBSD development team performs source-code audits of the core operating system in an effort to stamp out bugs, especially security-related bugs. There is also a strong cryptographic emphasis throughout the code in an attempt to protect and hide sensitive data. This has lead to an operating system that tends to be more secure out of the box.

However, like any operating system, the security of the host depends on the diligence of the operator. A heavily audited operating system such as OpenBSD can still be made vulnerable to simple attacks through misconfiguration or open policies. Host security is especially important to wireless stations, since the station computers are generally a weak and difficult link to manage in a wireless network.

OpenBSD Client Setup

OpenBSD shares features and architecture with some of the other free BSDs such as FreeBSD and NetBSD. OpenBSD's wireless support is no exception. OpenBSD has pulled functionality and code from FreeBSD wireless subsystem, and FreeBSD has pulled from OpenBSD as well. In general, running a secure OpenBSD workstation is similar to a FreeBSD workstation. However, this chapter will cover some important differences.

Unless otherwise noted, the examples in this chapter are from the OpenBSD 3.1 release. OpenBSD may be obtained from *http://www.openbsd.org/* and either purchased on CD or installed over the Internet.

Kernel Configuration

Like any other operating system, a secure host starts with a secure kernel configuration. If unneeded devices or options are included in your kernel configuration, you will not only have a bloated and slower kernel, but you may also open yourself up to attacks. The kernel should be configured using the Principle of Least Privilege. In short, if you do not need something in your kernel, do not add it! Also, an OpenBSD kernel can be configured with special options that can lead to a more secure machine. These options should be added when possible to help keep attackers out.

Wireless Kernel Configuration

In order to use wireless NICs, the kernel must be configured to support your wireless networking card. The process of compiling an OpenBSD kernel is outside the scope of this book. For more information on compiling a custom OpenBSD kernel, see *http://www.openbsd.org/faq/faq5.html* and the *options(4)* manual page.

When compiling an OpenBSD kernel, there are two different files that you may need to edit in order to add or remove all of the required options. The first configuration file, */usr/src/sys/conf/GENERIC*, contains options that are common across all the architectures OpenBSD can run on. OpenBSD has been ported to many platforms, including i386, Sparc, PowerPC, and VAX. Some options, such as firewalling and IPv6 support, are shared between all the platforms, and therefore when you change an option in */usr/src/sys/conf/GENERIC*, it will be reflected in any kernel you build for any platform.

The second file is the platform-specific file found in */usr/src/sys/arch/<arch type>/ conf/*. The *<arch type>* is whatever architecture you're running on, which in most cases is i386. There is a GENERIC file in the architecture specific directory. You may edit this file directly or copy it to a new name, such as the hostname of your machine in all caps, for editing.

Your wireless card will probably be either PCI-based or PCMCIA-based. Add the appropriate options and devices to your architecture-specific configuration file:

```
# PCI PCMCIA controllers
pcic*   at pci? dev? function ?

# PCMCIA bus support
pcmcia* at pcic? controller ? socket ?
pcmcia* at tcic? controller ? socket ?
```

You must then add the proper devices for your particular wireless card. The wi driver works with Prism II–based cards as well as Hermes cards such as the Orinoco Silver. The an driver works with the Cisco wireless cards. Add the correct driver for your card. Note that there are different configuration lines depending on whether your card is PCI or PCMCIA based:

```
wi*     at pci? dev ? function ?        # WaveLAN IEEE 802.11DS
wi*     at pcmcia? function ?           # WaveLAN IEEE 802.11DS
an*     at pci? dev ? function ?        # Aironet IEEE 802.11DS
an*     at pcmcia? function ?           # Aironet IEEE 802.11DS
```

Now that you have support for your wireless cards, remove support for anything you do not need. For example, the GENERIC configuration file has many SCSI controllers and ISA network cards turned on by default. Comment out any devices you do not have. Once you have stripped down both the architecture-specific configuration file and the global file, compile your kernel according to the instructions on the OpenBSD web site. Verify your machine is operating as you expect it to. Once you have a functioning, bare-bones kernel, continue on to the security-specific configuration.

Security Kernel Configuration

The OpenBSD development teams place security above almost all else. Because of this, there are many security-specific options that you can and should compile into your kernel. Most of these options are in the global kernel configuration file that is found in */usr/src/sys/conf/GENERIC*.

OpenBSD has a cryptographic framework that allows drivers to hook into cryptographic services provided by the kernel. The IPsec implementation relies heavily upon the cryptographic framework. If you plan on using IPsec, enable this support with the following option:

```
option          CRYPTO          # Cryptographic framework
```

If you plan to use IPsec to secure your traffic, you will need to compile in IPsec support:

```
option          IPSEC           # IPsec
```

OpenBSD's firewall is provided a mechanism called packet filter (*pf*). *pf* provides a device (*/dev/pf*) to allow userland control of the firewall. Through */dev/pf* you can issue *ioctl* calls to add and remove rulesets, gather statistics on the firewall, and enable or disable the firewall completely. Through the use of *pflog*, *pf* can also provide packets to userland processes through a pseudo-interface called *pflog*. A firewall ruleset can log all denied packets to a *pflog* interface (such as *pflog0*) and a sniffer program such as *tcpdump* can monitor all the logged traffic. You should enable both *pf* and *pflog*:

```
pseudo-device   pf      1       # packet filter
pseudo-device   pflog   1       # pf log if
```

Finally, you should enable the ability to promiscuously sniff traffic from local interfaces. This ability can help greatly in debugging network problems and in using network-monitoring tools. This is accomplished through the use of a Berkeley Packet Filter (*bpfilter*). *bpfilter* will create a certain number of devices that will limit the number of connections processes can make to promiscuous interfaces. For example, if you have four different interfaces, then you will probably want four *bpfilter* instances so you can sniff on all interfaces at once:

```
pseudo-device   bpfilter 4      # packet filter
```

Card Configuration

There are several different ways to manipulate the wireless network card once the system is online. For Prism II and Hermes-based cards, the *wicontrol* utility can be used to configure wireless specific parameters. For Cisco Aironet cards the *ancontrol* utility is used instead. Some wireless capability has been added for all chipsets into the standard *ifconfig* utility. However you choose to configure your wireless network, you must be sure you configure your IP-specific parameters as well.

The following parameters are the more commonly used features of *wicontrol*. For a complete list, please see the *wicontrol* manual page.

`interface`
> This is the interface that *wicontrol* should operate on. If no interface is specified, wi0 is assumed. If no other flags are passed to *wicontrol*, *wicontrol* will print out the existing configuration and statistics of the interface.

`-n network name`
> This parameter specifies the name of the service set to join. In infrastructure mode, this would be the ESSID and in IBSS mode this would be the SSID of the network you wish to join. An empty string instructs the card to associate to the strongest available service set.

`-s station name`
> The station name is the value your station is to be known by on the network. Certain diagnostic and monitoring utilities will attempt to determine the station name in an effort to uniquely identify the end host. This is not required and should not be set.

`-f channel`
> This parameter indicates what channel the card should use to communicate with the access point. This value must be the same as the access point's channel or else association will not be possible. If no channel is specified, the card will scan all channels in an attempt to find an available access point.

`-p port type`
> This specifies the type of network to join. A value of 1 or bss will cause the card to only associate to infrastructure mode access points. A value of 4 or ibss will cause the card to operate in ad-hoc mode.

`-k key [ -v 1|2|3|4 ]`
> This parameter controls the various WEP keys used by the station to authenticate and encrypt traffic to the access point. key can be entered either as decimal (e.g., secrt) or as hexadecimal (e.g., 0x0123456789). The numbers following the key indicate which key index the specified key should be placed in. The WEP specification allows for four different keys to be stored for use in various key rotation strategies. If the –v flag is not specified, the first index is assumed.

-T 1|2|3|4

>This parameter specifies the index of the WEP key to use for encrypting transmitted frames.

For example, to configure your wi0 interface to associate to the ESSID Example using the WEP key secrt, issue the following command:

```
wicontrol wi0 -n Example -k secrt
```

To display statistics and configuration parameters of the wi0 interface, run the following command:

```
bash-2.05a# wicontrol wi0
NIC serial number:                      [ 99SA01000000 ]
Station name:                           [ WaveLAN/IEEE node ]
SSID for IBSS creation:                 [ IBSS ]
Current netname (SSID):                 [ Example ]
Desired netname (SSID):                 [ Example ]
Current BSSID:                          [ 00:02:2d:04:3d:5d ]
Channel list:                           [ 2047 ]
IBSS channel:                           [ 11 ]
Current channel:                        [ 1 ]
Comms quality/signal/noise:             [ 51 98 0 ]
Promiscuous mode:                       [ Off ]
Port type (1=BSS, 3=ad-hoc, 6=Host AP): [ 1 ]
MAC address:                            [ 00:04:e2:36:68:02 ]
Etc......
```

The *ancontrol* utility for the Cisco cards is similar to the *wicontrol* utility. Unfortunately the options passed to the different utilities are different. Again, the options discussed below are not a complete list of all possible options that can be passed to *ancontrol*. For the complete list and explanation, please see the *ancontrol* manual page.

interface

>This is the interface that *ancontrol* should operate on. If no interface is specified, wi0 is assumed. If no other flags are passed to *wicontrol*, *wicontrol* will print out the existing configuration and statistics of the interface.

[-v 1|2|3] -n ssid

>These options work in tandem to allow you to specify a hierarchy of service sets to join. The card will attempt to associate to the SSID specified in the first index, then the second, and finally the third. If the –v option is not used, the specified SSID is placed in the first index location.

-l station name

>The station name is the value your station is to be known by on the network. Certain diagnostic and monitoring utilities will attempt to determine the station name in an effort to uniquely identify the end host. This is not required and should not be set.

-c *channel*
> This parameter indicates what channel the card should use to communicate with the access point. This value must be the same as the access point's channel or else association will not be possible. If no channel is specified, the card will scan all channels in an attempt to find an available access point.

-o *0|1*
> This option specifies the network mode the card will attempt to join. A value of 0 instructs the card to join an ad-hoc network. A value of 1 will cause the card to participate in infrastructure mode networks.

-v *0|1|2|3|4|5|6|7* -k *key*
> These options work together to specify the WEP keys the card will use to communicate with. The *ancontrol* can only have four keys configured at a time. The even indexed keys are considered "permanent" and are stored in NVRAM on the card. The odd number keys are "temporary" and are stored in volatile memory. key can be entered either as decimal (e.g., secrt) or as hexadecimal (e.g., 0x0123456789). Unless the −e flag is used to specify the key to use to transmit, *ancontrol* will use the most recently entered key.

-e *0|1|2|3*
> This is the index of the WEP key to use to transmit encrypted frames.

-v *1|2|3|4* -a *AP*
> This option allows you to specify the MAC addresses of the preferred access points. The MAC address must be entered as six hexadecimal values separated by colons. By providing MAC addresses for your access points, your provide some level of protection from an attacker standing up an access point claiming to be part of your service set and hijacking your association.

For example, to configure your an0 interface to associate to the ESSID Example using the WEP key secrt, issue the following command:

```
ancontrol −n Example −v 0 −k secrt
```

Startup Configuration

The wireless card needs to be properly initialized and configured at boot time to avoid having to hand configure the interface after each reboot. In OpenBSD, each interface has a file in hostname named *hostname.<interface>* that contains information regarding the configuration of the interface. For instance, the first Prism-based interface on a host will be controlled by a file called *hostname.wi0*.

The file can specify basic IP configuration information as well as execute arbitrary commands to configure other aspects of the interface. At the most basic level, the IP configuration takes the following form:

```
addr_family [alias] address netmask broadcast_address options
```

addr_family can be *inet*, *inet6*, or *dhcp*. For the case of DHCP with no required options, the options fields should be filed in with the string NONE. To execute commands within the file, precede the command with an exclamation point. For example, to configure the first Prism-based controller with an IP address of 192.168.0.248 on a class C network with a default gateway and associating to an SSID of Example, use the following file:

```
inet 192.168.0.248 255.255.255.0 192.168.0.255
!route add default 192.168.0.1
!wicontrol \$if -n Example
```

The *hostname.interface* file is very flexible and powerful. For a complete discussion of the structure of this file, see the *hostname.if* manual page.

OS Protection

A secure kernel and properly configured network interfaces are only part of configuring a secure station. There are various parts of the operating system that you must secure to protect yourself from attackers. This includes configuring a host-based firewall, removing unneeded services being started at boot time, and setting static ARP entries to avoid ARP spoofing attacks.

Firewall Configuration

A firewall configuration on a wireless client is generally straightforward. Almost all connections will be outbound from the host. Unless you are running externally accessible services such as a web or *ssh* server, there should never be a connection attempt from outside hosts.

The firewall configuration is stored in */etc/pf.conf*. The file contains directives that will be passed to the packet filter at boot time.

Here is an simple *pf.conf* that should work on most client installations. If you require a more advanced firewall setup or would like a more complete discussion of *pf*, see "Building the Firewall Rules" in Chapter 13 or read the *pf.conf* manual page.

```
# Simple client pf.conf
oif = "wi0"
onet = "192.168.0.0"
omask = "255.255.255.0"
oip = "192.168.0.248"
# block by default
block in log all
# Let loopback traffic through
pass out quick on lo0 all
pass in quick on lo0 all
# keep windows hosts from filling your logs
block in quick on $oif proto tcp from any to any port 136 >< 140
# keep broadcasts from filling your logs
```

```
block in quick on $oif inet from any to { 255.255.255.255, 192.168.0.255 }
# allow everything outbound
pass out quick on $oif all keep state
```

Make sure you have *pf* support compiled into your kernel and set pf=YES in */etc/rc. conf* to cause the firewall to be enabled at boot time. This is a very simple firewall configuration. However, in a hostile wireless environment, keeping things simple may make the difference between keeping attackers off your machine and being the weakest link in the network.

Disable Unneeded Services

Unneeded services running on a machine are a liability. An unneeded service becomes a forgotten service. And a vulnerability discovered in a forgotten service can quickly lead to a compromise. By removing unneeded services from your machine, you make administration easier and increase the security of the host.

In a default OpenBSD install, there are two major places where services are launched. The standard *inetd* facility controls services such as telnet, ftp, chargen, etc. These services are configured in */etc/inetd.conf*. Edit this file and comment out any services you do not require. In general, *ssh* will provide all required remote services so you should be able to comment out everything in *inetd.conf*.

The other source of many services is */etc/rc.conf*. Again, edit this file and examine it for any services you do not need. Turn services off by setting the option to NO. For example, disable portmapper by changing:

```
portmap=YES            # almost always needed
```

to this:

```
portmap=NO             # almost always needed
```

Restart your machine for these changes to take effect. Verify the machine acts as you anticipate and you have not disabled services in error.

Static ARP Entries

As documented in "ARP Poisoning" in Chapter 2, there is a real threat from man-in-the-middle attacks due to ARP poisoning. A malicious user may be able to convince your workstation that her host is the gateway by forging spoofed packets. By putting a static ARP entry on your host, the effectiveness of this attack is minimized.

Through the *ancontrol* utility, Cisco cards can be configured to only associate with authorized MAC addresses. Whenever possible, this filtering should be configured. Authorized access point MAC address filtering in combination with static ARP entries for your layer 3 gateway will prevent many of the attacks that can be launched at layer 2.

Static ARP entries override any dynamic information received over the network. If you are always using the same gateway (i.e., you are not roaming around to different layer 3 wireless networks) you can put a script in /etc called staticarp.sh to hard code the ARP entry:

```
#!/bin/sh
# staticarp.sh
# This script will set static arp entries for OpenBSD
# Add the ARP entry for the gateway

    echo -n ' adding gateway arp'
    /usr/sbin/arp -d <gatewayIP>
    /usr/sbin/arp -s <gatewayIP> <gatewayMAC> permanent
```

Make sure you make this shell script executable. In order to run this file at boot time, add the following lines to /etc/rc.local:

```
# Set static ARP entries for gateway
if [ -f /etc/staticarp.sh ]; then
      . /etc/staticarp.sh
fi
```

After your next reboot, verify the script has executed correctly by using the arp command:

```
bash-2.05a# arp -an
? (192.168.0.1) at 00:02:2d:08:5b:30 permanent static
? (192.168.0.2) at 00:10:5a:a7:09:2a
```

The word permanent indicates that no network traffic including malicious ARPs from other hosts will override this static entry.

Audit Logging

Due to OpenBSD's similarities to FreeBSD, configuring logging and log file monitoring is almost identical under both operating systems. For a complete discussion of auditing under FreeBSD, see "Audit Logging" in Chapter 4.

## CHAPTER 7

Mac OS X Station Security

Apple's Mac OS X operating system has been rapidly gaining in popularity among security professionals. This can most likely be attributed to its excellent GUI, BSD underpinnings, and increased focus on security features. Apple has taken a proactive stance in developing a more secure OS, and is working hand-in-hand with the BSD community to explore secure standards for the BSD family of operating systems.

Mac OS X Setup

The underlying structure of Mac OS X uses many BSD-derived components. Because of this, the configuration, scripts, and firewall are very similar to FreeBSD. File paths are often different, but the concepts remain the same. The examples and walk-throughs in this chapter work on both Mac OS X Versions 10.1 and 10.2.

Kernel Configuration

Mac OS X installs with a pre-compiled kernel that contains support for everything needed to use the OS as a wireless client. There is no need to compile a custom kernel, but if you do want to experiment with different options for the kernel, visit *http://www.opendarwin.org* to get started. The Mac OS X kernel builds are derived from the OpenDarwin kernel but changed somewhat before release by Apple. Building a custom kernel is a path for the more daring, and technical, user.

Card Configuration

Support for the Apple AirPort wireless card is completely integrated into Mac OS X. Configuration is accomplished through the System Preferences dialog boxes. The settings and options are primarily contained in two tabs of the Network section of System Preferences.

Figure 7-1 shows the AirPort configuration tab. The AirPort ID is the MAC address of the wireless card in the computer. The series of options below determine the way the OS will select which wireless network to join at startup or when to come out of a standby mode. The first option joins the network with the strongest signal. The second option will rejoin a recently used network. This option has a checkbox to remember network passwords, which is how Mac OS X refers to WEP keys. The final option restricts the computer to only connecting to a specified network SSID. (The SSID is Wireless in this example.)

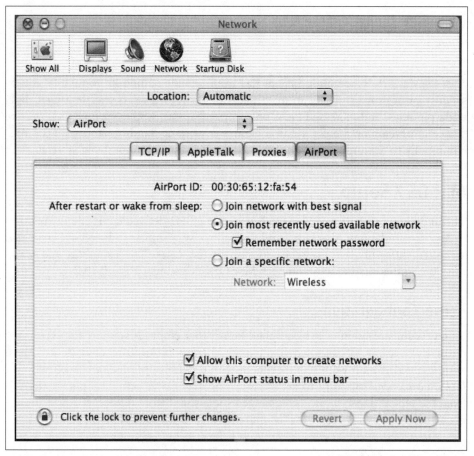

Figure 7-1. AirPort card configuration tab

There are two checkboxes at the bottom of the tab. The first enables the creation of IBSS networks, operating in peer-to-peer mode between workstations. The second adds an icon (Figure 7-2) to the menu bar to display the status of the network connection and provide a small drop-down menu of common actions.

Figure 7-2. AirPort status icon on menu bar (second from left)

Also in the Network section of System Preferences is a tab for the wireless card TCP/IP settings. An example of this tab is shown in Figure 7-3. Make sure you select your wireless card in the Show drop-down list before changing settings. The Configure setting will determine whether DHCP or static address information is to be used. If static settings are used, the rest of the fields in the tab can be used to set the network configuration.

Figure 7-3. TCP/IP networking configuration tab

Besides showing whether the AirPort is connected to a wireless network, the status icon in Figure 7-2 also provides a menu of common actions. All the detected SSIDs of nearby wireless networks are displayed on the menu; clicking on one will cause the computer to attempt to connect. If the network is closed (requires WEP), a dialog box prompting for the password (WEP key) will appear. The WEP key should be entered in hexadecimal notation, not as regular characters.

There is also a choice titled Create Network. After selecting this, a dialog box will request a network name (SSID), password (WEP key), and channel. The wireless card will create an IBSS network with these settings.

AirPort Access Point Utilities

Mac OS X includes two programs to help in configuring the Apple AirPort AP. If you are using an AirPort AP, the AirPort Admin Utility and AirPort Setup Assistant, which are both located in the Utilities folder, can be used to remotely configure the AP. Since these tools are SNMP based, you may also have (limited) success using them to configure other APs.

OS Protection

In addition to securing the wireless connection itself, it is important to lock down the rest of the services running on the computer. Unneeded services should be disabled, and a firewall should be established to protect the host. It is also worthwhile to set up a static ARP address for the gateway to protect against man-in-the-middle attacks and automate the monitoring of logs.

Disable Unneeded Services

The System Preferences section titled Sharing controls what services will be run on the system. The Services tab, shown in Figure 7-4, controls what file-sharing services will be started on the system. Uncheck any of these you do not need to use. Remote Login is one service you might want to use; it provides a SSH login server to allow remote shell access.

Firewall Configuration

The Firewall tab of the Sharing configuration allows groups of ports to be filtered. Disable access to all services, unless you need to allow access. In the example shown in Figure 7-5, the firewall is off.

You can enable the limited firewalling configuration provided in this GUI setup program by pressing the Start button. If you want to use a more complicated set of filtering rules, it requires creating a script to run at system startup.

If you don't use the GUI firewall configuration, you need to enable the automatic running of a script as a startup item by the *SystemStarter* program. First, create the directory */System/Library/StartupItems/Firewall*. In this directory, place the file

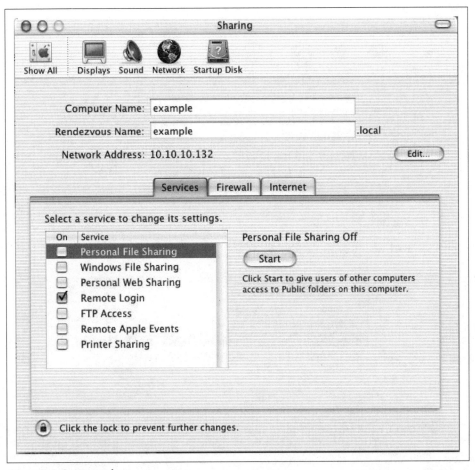

Figure 7-4. Services tab

/System/Library/StartupItems/Firewall/StartupParameters.plist. This file describes the services provided by the startup item, and should contain the following:

```
{
  Description    = "Firewall";
  Provides       = ("Firewall");
  Requires       = ("Network");
  OrderPreference = "Late";
  Messages =
  {
    start = "Starting firewall";
    stop  = "Stopping firewall";
  };
}
```

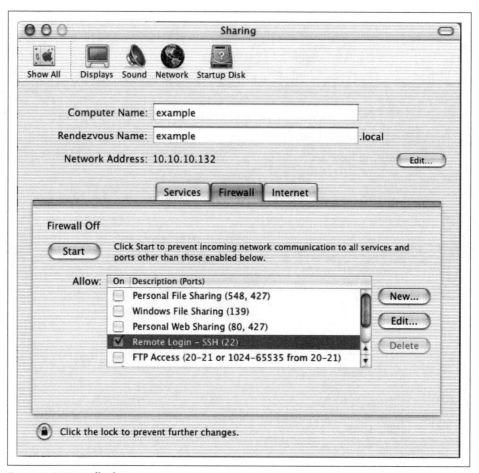

Figure 7-5. Firewall tab

The main script that starts the firewall should have the same name as the directory it lives in. This file will be called */System/Library/StartupItems/Firewall/Firewall*. It writes a log message and then starts a monitoring script. The Firewall script is:

```
#!/bin/sh

##
# Firewall
##

. /etc/rc.common

ConsoleMessage "Starting Firewall"

/usr/local/sbin/fwmon &
echo $! > /var/run/fwmon.pid
```

The monitoring script called by Firewall is */usr/local/sbin/fwmon*. This script will listen for events signaling a change in IP addresses or the restart of network adapters. When one of those events is received, it will call */usr/local/sbin/firewall.sh* to reload the ruleset. Create this file with the following contents:

```sh
#!/bin/sh

SystemLog( )
{
    local Message="$*"

    logger -it fwmon "${Message}"
}

UpdateFirewall( )
{
    /usr/local/sbin/firewall.sh > /dev/null
    for iface in `ifconfig -lu`; do
    case "${iface}" in
        ppp*)
            ifconfig ${iface} mtu 1448
            ;;
    esac
    done
}

SystemLog "Firewall monitoring started"
UpdateFirewall

while true
do
    /usr/sbin/scutil -p <<-SC_SCRIPT > /dev/null
        open
        n.add State:/Network/Global/IPv4
        n.wait
        close
    SC_SCRIPT

    sleep 3
    SystemLog "IP Address added, removed or changed.  Reconfiguring firewall."
    UpdateFirewall
done

exit 0
```

The final script is */usr/local/sbin/firewall.sh* itself. This file contains the rules that will be assigned to each interface in the machine. It should contain:

```sh
#!/bin/sh

ipfw=ipfw

AddRule( )
{
```

```
    local rule="$*"

    ${ipfw} add ${rule} via ${iface} > /dev/null
}

LoopbackFirewall()
{
    AddRule allow all from any to any
}

DefaultFirewall()
{
    # Prevent spoofing of the loopback network
    AddRule deny log all from any to 127.0.0.0/8

        # Allow DHCP traffic
        AddRule allow udp from any 67 to any 67
        AddRule allow udp from any 67 to any 68
        AddRule allow udp from any 68 to any 67
        AddRule allow udp from any 68 to any 68

    # Prevent bogus addresses
    AddRule deny log all from 0.0.0.0/8 to any in
    AddRule deny log all from 169.254.0.0/16 to any in
    AddRule deny log all from 192.0.2.0/24 to any in
    AddRule deny log all from 224.0.0.0/4 to any in
    AddRule deny log all from 240.0.0.0/4 to any in
    AddRule deny log all from any to 0.0.0.0/8 in
    AddRule deny log all from any to 169.254.0.0/16 in
    AddRule deny log all from any to 192.0.2.0/24 in
    AddRule deny log all from any to 224.0.0.0/4 in
    AddRule deny log all from any to 240.0.0.0/4 in

    # Allow established connections to persist - DANGEROUS, but unavoidable
    # since ipfw sadly does not keep state as of OS X 10.1.
    AddRule allow tcp from any to any established

    # Allow certain ICMP traffic (ping and required stuff)
    AddRule allow icmp from any to any icmptypes 0,3,4,8,11,12

    # Allow DNS traffic in both directions
    AddRule allow udp from any 53 to ${ipaddr} in
    AddRule allow udp from ${ipaddr} to any 53 out

    # Refuse AUTH requests.  Reject the connection rather than deny it so
    # that we don't have to wait for timeouts, etc.
    AddRule reject tcp from any to any 113

    # Allow traffic outgoing from this machine
    AddRule allow tcp from ${ipaddr} to any out
    AddRule allow udp from ${ipaddr} to any out

    # If we're on our home network, allow SMB traffic
    if [ "${domain}" == "yourhomedomainhere.com" ]; then
        AddRule allow tcp from ${ipaddr}:${netmask} 137-139 to any in
```

```
        AddRule allow udp from ${ipaddr}:${netmask} 137-139 to any in
        AddRule allow tcp from ${ipaddr} to ${ipaddr}:${netmask} 137-139 out
        AddRule allow udp from ${ipaddr} to ${ipaddr}:${netmask} 137-139 out
    fi

    # Finally, a default rule to deny
    AddRule deny log ip from any to any
}

# Ensure logging is enabled in the kernel
if [ `/usr/sbin/sysctl -n net.inet.ip.fw.verbose` == 0 ]; then
    /usr/sbin/sysctl -w net.inet.ip.fw.verbose=1 > /dev/null
fi

# Cleanup any mess that may have been left behind from previous invocations
# or manual use of the firewalling interface.
${ipfw} -f flush > /dev/null

# Check the nameserver configuration to find out what our domain is
read junk domain < /etc/resolv.conf

for iface in `ifconfig -lu`; do
    # Get the ip address assigned to the interface.  If there is none, then
    # the interface isn't truly active and we skip it.
    line=`ifconfig ${iface} | grep -E '^[[:space:]]+inet[[:space:]]+.*$'`
    if [ -z "${line}" ]; then
        continue
    fi
    echo "${line}" | read junk ipaddr junk netmask junk

    case "${iface}" in
        lo*)
            LoopbackFirewall
            ;;
        *)
            DefaultFirewall
            ;;
    esac
done

exit 0
```

After creating the scripts, use the following commands to ensure that the files are owned by the proper user and that the three script files are set executable with *chmod*:

```
# chown root:admin /Library/StartupItems/StaticArp/*
# chown root:admin /usr/local/sbin/firewall.sh
# chown root:admin /usr/local/sbin/fwmon
# chmod 755 /Library/StartupItems/StaticArp/StaticArp
# chmod 755 /usr/local/sbin/firewall.sh
# chmod 755 /usr/local/sbin/fwmon
```

The firewall will start upon the next reboot, or it can be started immediately with:

```
# SystemStarter start Firewall
```

Static ARP Entries

To protect against ARP man-in-the-middle attacks, which are described in Chapter 2, set static ARP entries using a startup item script similar to the one described for the firewall.

Create the directory */System/Library/StartupItems/StaticARP*, and place the file */System/Library/StartupItems/StaticARP/StartupParameters.plist* in there with the following contents:

```
{
  Description     = "Static ARP";
  Provides        = ("StaticARP");
  Requires        = ("Network");
  OrderPreference = "Late";
  Messages =
  {
    start = "Starting Static ARP";
    stop  = "Stopping Static ARP";
  };
}
```

The script */System/Library/StartupItems/StaticARP/StaticARP* will add the ARP entry for the gateway when it is started and remove it when stopped. Insert the correct gateway IP and MAC address into the listing below, and place in the file:

```
#!/bin/sh

##
# StaticArp
##

. /etc/rc.common

case "$1" in
    start)
        ConsoleMessage "Adding static ARP entry for gateway"
        /usr/sbin/arp -s <gatewayIP> <gatewayMAC>
    ;;

    stop)
        ConsoleMessage "Deleting static ARP entry for gateway"
        /usr/sbin/arp -d <gatewayIP>
    ;;
esac
```

Set the ownership of these two files, and make the script executable using these commands:

```
# chown root:admin /Library/StartupItems/StaticARP/*
```

```
# chmod 755 /Library/StartupItems/StaticARP/StaticARP
```

The static ARP entries will be set upon the next reboot, or they can be set immediately with:

```
# SystemStarter start StaticARP
```

To clear the static ARP entries, use the following command:

```
# SystemStarter stop StaticARP
```

Audit Logging

The messages generated by the firewall and other services are written to the file */var/log/System.log* under Mac OS X. Make sure to review these logs on a regular basis to look for evidence of attacks or compromise. A monitoring tool, such as *swatch*, can help by automating the monitoring.

If you want to use *swatch* as described in Chapter 4, you must start it with the following command:

```
swatch –tail-file=/var/log/System.log --config-file=swatch.config
```

This will tell *swatch* the path to the *System.log* file, so it knows where to find the logs on Mac OS X. See "Audit Logging" in Chapter 4 for more information on this tool.

## CHAPTER 8

Windows Station Security

Many people have computers that use Windows, especially when it comes to company laptops. This chapter is a brief description of the basic steps to secure a Windows computer using a wireless connection.

Windows Client Setup

All wireless cards come with Windows drivers; getting a wireless card functioning under Windows usually involves little more than installing the supplied drivers. It is probably a good idea to download the latest drivers from the manufacturer's web site, along with any firmware revisions for the card. Configure the network settings for the card in the Network Properties control panel, and use either DHCP or the IP, netmask, etc. that you have decided upon.

OS Protection

The next thing you should do is download the latest service pack and security patches from Microsoft for the version of Windows you are using. Check Microsoft's site for new patches on a regular basis, or use the Windows Update tool. New patches are released quite frequently.

Beyond this, you should look into the various techniques for locking down Windows. The NSA has published guides for Windows 2000 and Windows NT that are available at *http://nsa1.www.conxion.com/*. Windows 95, 98, and ME were not designed for secure operation in a networked environment, and it's probably best to use a more recent version of Windows if possible. Microsoft's resources on security are all indexed at *http://www.microsoft.com/security* and *http://www.microsoft.com/windowsxp/security*.

Virus Protection

One of the primary security hazards to Windows computers is infection with a virus, Trojan, or worm. Run anti-virus software. There is no excuse for not doing this when using Windows. Ensure that the anti-virus software's virus database is regularly updated; use an automatic update system if supported by the software.

Firewall

Windows, with the exception of Windows XP, does not come with a built-in firewall. There are many firewall products on the market that provide various types of protection. Some integrate virus checking and other security features. Shop around and read reviews to find one that meets your needs. (Our current favorite is Tiny Personal Firewall. You can download it at *http://www.tinysoftware.com*.)

The actual firewall rules for Windows are going to be similar in behavior to what was described for other client OSes in previous chapters. The only new connections should be outbound from the host; there should be no inbound connection requests. If you do have a server running on your client, you will need to modify your firewall configuration appropriately. How to actually create the rules is going to depend on which firewall you decide to use. (Be aware that many Windows VPN clients and firewalls do not interoperate well and may not be usable simultaneously.)

With Windows, it isn't a good idea to use file sharing, the Network Neighborhood (protocol SMB/CIFS), over a wireless network. To do so invites all sorts of trouble through password compromise and snooped files. This can be blocked by using the firewall to filter out ports 135 through 139 for both TCP and UDP. If you are not going to use file or printing sharing at all, it is probably best to disable and uninstall sharing through the network properties dialog box.

Static ARP

Just like with any other OS, ARP poisoning is a danger. Unfortunately, with most versions of Windows there is not much you can do about it.

Static ARP entries on Windows are set by the command:

```
arp -s <IP> <MAC>
```

This will bind the given IP to the given MAC hardware address.

Where this static ARP entry differs in behavior from Linux and the *BSD operating systems is in the definition of "static." On Windows, "static" means the entry will not time out. On Linux and *BSD, it means it will not time out and it will not be changed by ARP traffic from the network. Windows XP is the exception in the Windows family; its static ARP entries behave as they do under Linux and *BSD.

This means that even if you set a static ARP entry on Windows, an attacker who is forging ARP reply packets to misdirect your traffic will still succeed. (Unless you are running XP.)

Given this fact, it's only worth creating static ARP entries on Windows XP. Since the ARP table is cleared on reboot, place commands to create static ARP entries for your gateway computer in a batch file and run it on system startup.

Audit Logging

Pay attention to the audit logs Windows generates, especially the security log. Look out for failed user authentication attempts and other strange events that you didn't cause.

Also, pay attention to the logs generated by your firewall and anti-virus software. Try to refine your firewall logging settings to eliminate all of the noise from the automated scans of worms like *CodeRed* and *Nimda*. In the case of these two worms, this can be accomplished by not logging blocked TCP port 80 requests. After collecting a few weeks of logs, it should be apparent what kind of noise traffic you are receiving.

Secure Communication

It bears repeating one more time: No matter how strong your firewall is, no matter how solid your system configuration is, if you send your mail password in the clear across the network, you have subverted all the security built into your system. Secure communication is the keystone in client-side security. For a full discussion of secure communication mechanisms, see "Secure Communication" in Chapter 3.

## PART III

Access Point Security

A wireless access point can come in many shapes and sizes. There are commodity access points that can be purchased at your local computer store for around a hundred dollars. There are also industrial-quality access points sold by companies like Cisco Systems for thousands of dollars. Alternatively, through the hard work of open source developers, you can turn a Linux, FreeBSD, or OpenBSD host into an access point. Regardless of the type of access points you use, securing them is critical to the security of your entire network infrastructure. By using encryption, authentication, and proper monitoring, your access points will facilitate secure wireless communication.

## CHAPTER 9

Setting Up an Access Point

Access points come in all shapes and sizes. Most access points deployed today are firmware devices running a proprietary operating system. These access points are usually inexpensive yet reliable. Unfortunately, securing these access points can be a challenge as they have very few security-specific options and are generally not very flexible.

Linux, FreeBSD, and OpenBSD machines can be converted to access points with the proper drivers and configuration options. Access points running on general-purpose operating systems provide much more flexibility to meet the challenges of specific security requirements. However, like any host, these machines must be properly secured and monitored to prevent attackers from compromising the host or the network.

This chapter will show you general techniques for locking down access points for secure use. It will also show you how to setup Linux, FreeBSD, and OpenBSD to run in *HostAP* mode, turning the machine into a full-fledged access point.

 Mac OS X also has a feature called Airport Software Base Station. Enabling this provides a peer-to-peer 802.11b network, not a BSS network like a regular AP or *HostAP* as discussed in this chapter.

General Access Point Security

Several security features are common across most access point vendors. The manner in which these features are configured vary from vendor to vendor. Please consult the documentation that came with your access point to determine the correct method. None of the features mentioned offer are bulletproof security, but they raise the bar substantially for an attacker.

WEP Keys

Even though the crypto underlying WEP has been broken, it is still important to configure WEP for several reasons. Primarily, it serves as a reasonably strong barrier against the casual attacker. Raw 802.11 frames can be captured via *tcpdump* on almost any platform. Without WEP, it is trivial to sniff traffic, determine layer 3 gateways, and gain access to the network. By enabling WEP, you are forcing the attacker to crack your WEP key to accomplish the same tasks. The tools used to crack WEP are substantially more difficult to use than *tcpdump*, as well as take a fair bit of time to run. A person will likely not sit in a car in your parking lot for the many hours it will take to capture enough traffic to crack your WEP encryption.

Secondly, there may be legal reasons why running WEP is a good idea. For the record, the authors are not lawyers, however, based on our years of work in the security field we have read about enough legal battles to know a good legal practice when we see it. Typically a systems operator must place a "No Trespassing" sign of some nature on a resource to prevent a hacker from "accidentally" breaking into a system. With telnet, this can be accomplished with a login banner to the effect of "Authorized Users only. Unauthorized access will be logged and prosecuted." This is a clearly worded warning to would-be attackers that the system is private. In a court of law, this type of statement will remove an attacker's defense of ignorance. WEP is the wireless analog to a telnet login banner. By enabling WEP on your network, you are putting up a sign to attackers that your system is off limits and you have a reasonable expectation of privacy. If an attacker goes through the trouble of cracking your WEP key, then they are obviously aware they are breaking into a system that they have no right being in. In the event that you catch the attacker, your use of WEP may help in your prosecution.

When configuring WEP, always use 128-bit keys if possible. As time passes and WEP is refined, the key size will likely continue to increase. As a rule, use the largest key size your hardware can bear without performance impact.

Also, many WEP implementations allow for entry of four different WEP keys at one time. This allows you as an administrator to create a WEP key rotation policy. The frequency of key rotation is a function of the amount of data transmitted on the network, the number of users on the network, and the paranoia of the administrator.

Only one key can be used to transmit at any given time. However by entering four keys in, you can implement a key rotation schedule. For example, give your users four new keys at the first of the month. Tell the users to transmit with *key[0]* for the first week, then *key[1]* for the second, *key[2]* for the third, then *key[3]* for the fourth. The clients and AP can understand packets encrypted with any of the four keys so the users do not need to change their transmit keys at exactly the same time. If you want to force them to change, you can change the key at location X on the AP. At that point, the users who are still encrypting with *key[X]* are unable to talk on the network anymore. Generally, they will notice this problem and contact someone to get the new keys.

MAC Address Filtering

Most access points also have MAC address filtering capabilities. This feature can be configured in an open or closed manner. In an open MAC filter, the MAC addresses listed are prevented from accessing the network. In a closed MAC filter, only the listed addresses are allowed to access the network. A closed filter is the more secure option as only known cards are permitted. Keeping track of MAC addresses can be difficult in a network of any size. If you are planning to install a large network, you may be able to request cards from your wireless vendor with sequential MAC addresses to make filtering easier.

Many wireless cards on the market allow the MAC address to be changed by the user. This is usually a trivial change accessed via the driver GUI in Windows or *ifconfig* in Linux/FreeBSD. An attacker who is snooping your network for traffic could easily change his card's MAC address to match a host that he knows is currently allowed through the filter. Again, like WEP, MAC filtering has failings, but it continues to raise the bar.

Management Interfaces

Most access points offer several means of administration. Common administration access methods are through telnet, HTTP, or a serial/USB connection. Telnet administration should be avoided, and disabled if possible, since passwords will transit the network in the clear. If supported by the access point, limit administration traffic to the wired side of the network. For smaller networks, or when remote administration of access points is not needed, disable the online administration entirely and use the serial connection. Many access points have had security problems with their administration servers, so they should be disabled if you are not going to need to access them.

Log Host

Your access point may be able to log critical events to a central log host via *syslog*. Configure your access point to log to a central server (possibly your firewall) and examine what is logged. You may see events such as system restarts, failed authentication attempts, and new associations. Using *swatch* (as discussed in Chapter 4), you can monitor and alert on events you deem important. Examining associations can be especially useful and interesting. Individual users that are war-driving your access point will leave their first audit trail as they associate. Depending on your gateway auditing (discussed in Chapter 10), you will see even more footprints as they work their way out of your network.

Trap Host

Some access points will allow an SNMP trap host to be configured in place of a log host. A *trap* is an SNMP message caused by a critical event on the device. A trap will typically contain the same type of information has a log entry for an event logged via *syslog*. You may need to configure a password on your trap host and access point in order for the trap to be accepted by the trap host.

Authentication Methods

This option is called something different by almost every vendor. Basically it refers to the ability to require WEP authentication to access the network. An *open network* is a network that does not require any authentication at all. A station makes an association request and that request is granted. A *closed network* requires a WEP authenticated association. Without WEP, the requesting station is denied access. A *mixed* environment will allow unauthenticated or authenticated access to the network. A closed network is obviously the best choice for ensuring authentication of clients. However, you may need to run in mixed mode when troubleshooting station connectivity issues.

SNMP Monitoring

SNMP is a very powerful protocol for managing network-connected devices. Every firmware-based access point I have used, from the lowest priced consumer grade AP to expensive ISP quality kits, had some manner of SNMP interface. Most access points are configured either via an SNMP interface or a web interface. Even the access points with a web interface have had an SNMP system for remote monitoring.

SNMP employs the concept of *managers* and *agents*. *Managers* are centralized hosts that make SNMP requests to devices that run agents. The *agents* then process the request and send response data back to the manager. Agents can also send traps. An example of a SNMP manager and agents is shown in Figure 9-1.

SNMP Version 1 is the most commonly deployed version of SNMP. SNMP V1 allows for two types of access: read-only (RO) or read-write (RW). Community strings control the different types of access. Community strings are really nothing more than passwords to access the SNMP functionality of your device. Treat them as passwords and do not give them out to others. Also, be sure to change your default SNMP community string that ships with your access point. There are many web sites on the Internet that list the defaults settings for all known access points including community strings and IP addresses. By leaving your access point with the default

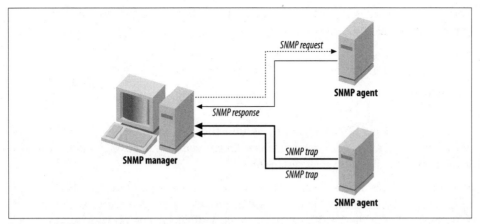

Figure 9-1. SNMP managers and agents

community string, you are practically inviting a war driver to change your AP's settings.

 SNMP V1 is a cleartext protocol. There is no inherent encryption to protect the traffic. Do *not* manage your wireless access point from the wireless interface. By managing the AP through the wired interface, you greatly reduce the chances of someone intercepting your community string.

The type of information that a manager can get and set on a remote device is stored in the Management Information Base (MIB). A MIB is a hierarchy of object descriptions, which is shown in Figure 9-2, that can be understood by an SNMP manager. Each object has a unique Object Identifier (OID), which can be expressed numerically via the object's descriptor or in alphanumeric strings via the object's name.

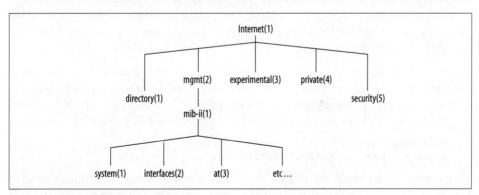

Figure 9-2. Part of the Internet MIB tree

For instance, there is an OID that represents the uptime of the system. This object can be represented by name or description:

Name
.iso.org.dod.internet.mgmt.mib-2.system.sysUpTime.0

Description
.1.3.6.1.2.1.1.3.0

Most of the existing SNMP managers assume they are dealing only with OIDs in the MIB-II tree. Therefore, *.iso.org.dod.internet.mgmt.mib-2.system.sysUpTime.0* can also be referenced as simply *system.sysUpTime.0*.

Vendors may have device-specific MIBs that can be loaded up into your SNMP manager. These MIBs typically define data that provides a customized view into proprietary parts of your device. These MIBs are generally available on your vendor's web site.

The 802.11 suite of protocols have their own MIB available from the IEEE. The MIB has subtrees to allow monitoring of the MAC and PHY layers as well as station-specific parameters. This MIB can be downloaded from the IEEE web site at *http://standards.ieee.org/getieee802/802.11.html*.

There are several different tools you can use for SNMP monitoring, depending on your requirements for scripting, ease of use, or expandability. At the very least you should experiment with each access point you purchase to see what information is available from your device.

net-snmp

net-snmp is a SNMP implementation that has been under development for many years. The project was formally known as *ucd-snmp*. *net-snmp* contains various utilities including an extensible SNMP agent, SNMP libraries, a suite of tools to get and set data on managed devices, trap tools, and a MIB browser. *net-snmp* is available from *http://net-snmp.sourceforge.net/*. Follow the directions in the current distribution for compiling and installing.

A complete discussion of *net-snmp* is outside the scope of this book. However, there are a few tools that are very useful when performing audits of access points. You can retrieve a specific OID using the *snmpget* command. To retrieve the uptime of a system at 192.168.0.2 with a community string of public, issue the following command:

```
bash$ snmpget 192.168.0.2 public system.sysUpTime.0
system.sysUpTime.0 = Timeticks: (196741426) 22 days, 18:30:14.26
```

This is great if you know the OID of the data you want. However, you may want to see all of the data the device is capable of returning. The *snmpwalk* command will walk an entire section of a MIB tree. For instance, to walk the IP MIB subtree on the same host, use the following:

```
bash$ snmpwalk 192.168.0.2 public ip
ip.ipForwarding.0 = not-forwarding(2)
ip.ipDefaultTTL.0 = 255
ip.ipInReceives.0 = Counter32: 113896
ip.ipInHdrErrors.0 = Counter32: 0
ip.ipInAddrErrors.0 = Counter32: 0
ip.ipForwDatagrams.0 = Counter32: 0
...
```

Walking a MIB tree can generate a lot of data, so you may want to redirect output to a file to examine. A vendor may expose a lot of information via a device's SNMP interface. Look for information such as association tables, DHCP lease information, and error rates. You should be able to generate Perl or shell scripts using *snmpget* to monitor values you deem important.

 The SNMP agent that runs on some access points may be buggy. We encountered quite a few access points that crashed when we walked the entire MIB tree. Not only is this annoying, but it can also be a denial-of-service attack vector for a malicious user. If your SNMP agent causes your AP to crash during a walk, contact your vendor's technical support. They are generally helpful in getting a fixed firmware version released.

Scotty/tkined

Scotty is a set of TCL extensions for network monitoring. *Scotty* allows for rapid network monitoring application development via a very robust suite of tools and APIs. *tkined* is a graphical framework for creating network maps and graphical monitoring tools. *tkined* is very extensible yet powerful out of the box. *Scotty/tkined* can be downloaded from *http://wwwhome.cs.utwente.nl/~schoenw/scotty/*. Follow the build and installation instructions that come with the current distribution.

tkined is a great tool for networking monitoring for a small network because it requires very little expertise to get up and running. However, because it is so extensible it can scale to handle very large networks. *tkined* can be configured to alarm on high and low thresholds, such as when an error rate on a wireless network becomes excessive. It can also graph time-dependant variables such as network utilization of free processor time. Figure 9-3 shows an access point with wireless network traffic being monitored and the SNMP configuration screen open.

Setting Up a Linux Access Point

Firmware devices are not the only machines that can serve as an access point. There is an 802.11 access point driver for Linux called *HostAP*. *HostAP* provides all of the standard access point functionality but you have the added benefit of a general-purpose operating system to allow you to create unique network architectures and security policies.

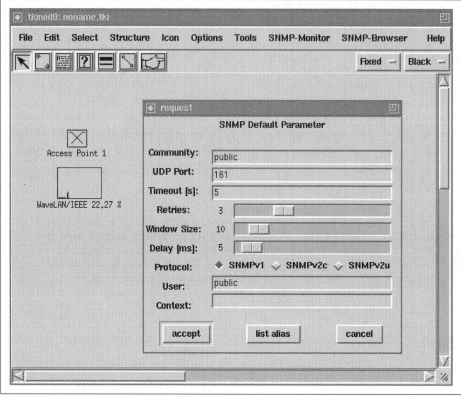

Figure 9-3. tkined in action

HostAP is designed to run on wireless cards that use Intersil's Prism chipset Version 2, 2.5, or 3. Cards based on this chipset include the D-Link DWL650, Netgear MA401, Compaq WL100, and the Linksys WMP11. Intersil, to date, is the only vendor to have released their radio specification to open source developers. It is possible that the *HostAP* driver will be ported to run on other chipsets in the future, so check the *HostAP* web site (*http://hostap.epitest.fi*) for equipment requirements. Most wireless cards on the market today do not specify the chipset used to drive the card. Check your vendor's web site or online lists of cards and their chipsets such as *http://www.personaltelco.net/index.cgi/Prism2Card*.

Installation of HostAP

In order to install *HostAP*, you will need a custom-built Linux 2.4 kernel and the kernel source code available. See "Wireless Kernel Configuration" in Chapter 5 for information on compiling your own kernel. If you are using the *pcmcia-cs* package, you will need its source code. You will also need to download the latest *HostAP* source code from *http://hostap.epitest.fi*.

Read the instructions that come with the distribution to determine how to install the *HostAP* driver. There are many different ways, and they all require your kernel to be compiled differently depending on the option you choose. You can compile *HostAP* as a loadable module for your existing kernel, as a replacement for the Prism drivers in the *pcmcia-cs* package, or as a replacement for your PLX drivers if you are using a PLX PCI-PCMCIA bridge. PLX bridges are common in desktop PCs that have PCMCIA card slots in them. They are very uncommon in laptops.

Once you get the *HostAP* driver installed per the instructions, your access point will appear as a *wlan* device:

```
bash# ifconfig wlan0
wlan0     Link encap:Ethernet  HWaddr 00:04:E2:36:68:02
          UP BROADCAST RUNNING MULTICAST  MTU:1500  Metric:1
          RX packets:597 errors:0 dropped:1720 overruns:0 frame:0
          TX packets:110440 errors:10 dropped:0 overruns:0 carrier:0
          collisions:0 txqueuelen:100
          RX bytes:7492 (7.3 Kb)  TX bytes:9070827 (8.6 Mb)
          Interrupt:3 Base address:0x2880
```

You cannot assign an IP address to the *wlan* device. However, you can create an Ethernet bridge to pass traffic between a wired network and a wireless network as a firmware access point would. Once you have created the bridge group, you can also assign an IP address to the bridge interface. This IP address will be accessible from both the wired and wireless networks.

You must have Ethernet bridging support compiled into your kernel:

```
CONFIG_BRIDGE=y
```

Once bridging support is compiled in, you may need to download the Ethernet bridging tools if they were not distributed with your core operating system. These tools can be obtained from *http://bridge.sourceforge.net/*. The tools have both a binary and a source distribution. Install whichever suits your needs.

The *brctl* command is used to control the activities of the bridge groups on the host. In order to bridge between the wired and wireless networks, you must first create the bridge group, then assign both interfaces to the group. Once that is done, you need to remove any existing IP address assignments and assign the address to the bridge interface. The following shell script can be run at startup to configure your access point to be a wired to wireless bridge:

```
#!/bin/sh
PATH=/usr/sbin:/sbin:/bin
# Check to see if bridge group 0 is already configured
ifconfig br0
if [ $? -ne 0 ]; then
    brctl addbr br0
    brctl addif br0 eth0
```

```
        brctl addif br0 wlan0
        ifconfig eth0 0.0.0.0
        ifconfig wlan0 0.0.0.0
        ifconfig br0 192.168.1.102 up
else
        echo "Bridge Group 0 already configured"
        exit 1;
fi
exit 0;
```

You should now be able to ping the bridge interface. Now you need to configure the access points wireless parameters. The *HostAP* driver is controlled by the *iwcontrol* and *iwpriv* commands. The following *iwcontrol* commands manipulate the *HostAP* driver in a similar manner to the methods documented in "Card Configuration" in Chapter 5, however in this case, they are configuring the access point for use by clients rather than configuring the client.

interface

This is the name of the interface to be configured. Typically, this value will be something like wlan0. If *iwconfig* is passed the interface name only and no other configuration parameters, it will return the current configuration of the wireless interface.

essid essid

This is the name of the Extended Service Set ID (ESSID) to create. This will be the value that stations will enter when prompted for their ESSID.

nwid nwid

This is the network ID. A network ID is a mechanism used to identify particular access points within an SSID. Many access points may have the same SSID and therefore provide service to the same network.

freq channel

This is the channel the access point will use to communicate with stations. The 802.11b PHY specification describes channels in the 2.4 GHz ISM band for use by 802.11b radios. In the U.S., there are 11 usable channels, while European countries have 14. The client must specify the same channel as the access point in order to be able to communicate with it.

key [wepkey] [index]

This flag controls all the WEP configuration options. The WEP key may be entered as hex (e.g., 0123-4567-89) or ASCII pre-pended with s: (e.g., s:secrt). Multiple keys can be entered and referenced by specifying an index value between 0 and 3.

For example, to set your *HostAP* driver to an ESSID of *linuxtest* running on channel 6 using WEP key secrt, issue the following command as root:

```
iwconfig wlan0 essid linuxtest freq 6 key s:secrt
```

These are not all of the commands supported by *iwcontrol*. See the documentation with the *HostAP* driver for more details.

The *iwpriv* tool is used to configure the portions of the access point that are not handled by *iwconfig*. The following are options that can be passed to *iwpriv*:

`interface monitor value`
>   This command controls the drivers' ability to snoop raw 802.11 frames. A value of 2 will sniff all 802.11 frames and allow user space programs to grab them. A value of 3 will grab all data received by the Prism chipset as well as all 802.11 frames and allow user space access. A value of 0 is normal, non-promiscuous access.

`interface maccmd value`
>   This sets the policy for the *HostAP* MAC address filtering. A value of 0 will allow all MAC addresses to connection, 1 will allow only listed MAC addresses to connect, and 2 will allow all MAC address but the ones listed to connect. A value or 3 will flush the existing MAC ACL, and 4 will disassociate all associated stations.

`interface addmac MAC addr`
>   This command will add the specified MAC address to the MAC ACL. The MAC address should be listed as a colon-separated list of hexadecimal bytes (i.e.,: `12:34:56:78:9a:bc`)

`interface delmac MAC addr`
>   This will remove the specified MAC address from the MAC ACL.

`interface kickmac MAC addr`
>   This will deassociate the specified MAC address from the network.

This is not an exhaustive list of commands that are handled by *iwpriv*. See the *HostAP* documentation for all possible options.

Once you have the *HostAP* driver configured as desired, there are various ways you can monitor the operations of the access point. The *HostAP* driver will provide information in the */proc/net* and */proc/net/prism2* directories. Using a tool such as *tkined* lets you monitor the contents of the files below and alarm on critical conditions such as excessive error rates or changes in core configurations. The following options allow you to monitor your files:

`/proc/net/prism2/interface/MAC address`
>   There is an entry in the prism2 directory for every associated MAC address. Each entry contains information regarding each station including supported bit rates, number of bytes transferred, signal levels, when the last association was, when the last authentication was, and when the last packet was received.

`/proc/net/prism2/interface/ap_control`
>   This file contains the MAC ACL policy type as well as the current MAC addresses listed in the ACL. These MAC addresses can be modified by *iwpriv*.

```
/proc/net/prism2/interface/ap_control
```
This file contains statistics about frames the access point has sent or received. This data includes the number of sent and received unicast packets, the number of excessive retries, undecryptable packets, and general discards.

The Linux *HostAP* driver provides a great deal of access-point functionality while continuing to offer all the flexibility of Linux. You can turn your access point into your network's IP gateway as well. For information on how to set up Linux gateways, see Chapter 11.

Setting Up a FreeBSD Access Point

Starting with FreeBSD 4.6, the default wireless driver (wi) has support for using the *HostAP* functionality of Intersil's Prism cards. The FreeBSD implementation is not as feature rich as the Linux implementation, yet. The *HostAP* projects in both Linux and FreeBSD development communities have received a great deal of attention. The features available in both implementations will continue to grow and become more robust.

When setting up a FreeBSD access point, it is advisable to start with a stripped down kernel configuration. The custom kernel you build must have the wi device configured. See "Wireless Kernel Configuration" and "Security Kernel Configuration" in Chapter 4 for a complete discussion on compiling a secure FreeBSD. There should be little difference between a client kernel and an access-point kernel. The principle of least privilege dictates that you should only compile in the features and devices you really need. The more unneeded options in your kernel, the greater the likely of your machine eventually being compromised.

Once you have a properly compiled kernel, configuring *HostAP* under FreeBSD is straightforward. FreeBSD has unified wireless control commands under the *ifconfig* utility. *HostAP* is enabled via a flag passed to *ifconfig*.

ifconfig in *HostAP* mode supports the following flags:

interface
    The name of the wireless interface to be managed.

ssid ssid
    The Service Set Identifier the access point will be identified by. This is the value stations will use to associate to this access point.

stationname name
    The name of the station the wireless card is installed in. This is an optional parameter used to identify different access points within an ESSID.

channel number
    The number of the channel the AP is to use. Under 802.11b networks governed by FCC regulations, this is a number between 1 and 11.

authmode mode

This is the authentication mode the stations must use when connecting to the access point. Values are none, open, and shared.

wepmode mode

This parameter indicates the method that stations will use WEP to form associations. off will allow the STA to be connected only to the access point as long as it does not use WEP. on forces the STA to use WEP for associations. When set to on, the access point will not allow client associations where the client allows non-WEP associations. mixed mode allows both WEP and non-WEP associations.

weptxkey index

The index is a value between 1 and 4 to indicate which WEP key is to be used for transmissions with the stations.

wepkey key | index:key

This specifies the value of the stored WEP keys. Four different keys can be stored by using index values between 1 and 4. The WEP key is specified as either an ASCII string or a hex value preceded by 0x.

mediaopts hostap

This parameter causes the card to go into HostAP mode and act as an 802.11 access point.

To put the host into *HostAP* mode with SSID *freebsdtest* on channel 6 with a WEP key of *secrt*, issue the following command as root:

```
ifconfig wi0 ssid freebsdtest channel 6 wepkey 1:secrt weptxkey 1 mediaopts hostap
```

The options passed to *ifconfig* can be placed into */etc/rc.conf* to cause *HostAP* mode to take effect at boot time:

```
ifconfig_wi0="channel 6 wepkey 1:secrt weptxkey 1 mediaopts hostap"
```

An IP address can be assigned to the wi interface using *ifconfig* to make the host a layer 3 gateway. However, using FreeBSD's built in Ethernet bridging functionality, you can make the machine act like a typical bridging access point. The kernel must have Ethernet bridging compiled in. This is accomplished by specifying option BRIDGE to the kernel configuration file.

Once bridging has been enabled, the wired and wireless interfaces must be placed into the bridge configuration:

```
bash# sysctl net.link.ether.bridge=1
bash# sysctl net.link.ether.bridge_cfg="wi0 <wired interface>"
bash# sysctl net.inet.ip.forwarding=1
```

Place these commands in a shell script in */usr/local/etc/rc.d* if you want the host to always boot as a bridging access point.

Unfortunately, since the FreeBSD *HostAP* implementation is very new, it is not as feature rich as its Linux counterpart. In particular, MAC address filtering is basically non-existent and there is no solid audit trail to watch. This is likely a temporary shortcoming as the extreme interest in *HostAP* development should lead to a greatly enhanced feature set in the near term. For the latest on FreeBSD's *HostAP* functions, MAC address filtering, and the audit trail, please visit this book's web site.

Setting Up an OpenBSD Access Point

OpenBSD introduced *HostAP*-mode functionality in Version 3.1. As with FreeBSD, the support comes native in the core operating system and not through a piece of third-party software. The FreeBSD and OpenBSD projects share a great deal of wireless code, and the *HostAP* functionality is no exception. Generally, the same capabilities that exist in FreeBSD exist in OpenBSD as well.

When setting up an OpenBSD access point, you should start out with a stripped-down and secured kernel. For a discussion on compiling a locked-down OpenBSD kernel, see "Kernel Configuration" in Chapter 6. There should be little difference between a client kernel and an access-point kernel. Both devices are in vulnerable locations on the network and should be treated the same.

At this time, *HostAP* mode is only available on Prism-based cards. Be sure you are using a Prism card and that you have the Prism driver (wi) compiled into your kernel. This section describes how to make a bridging access point. This will allow devices on the wired and wireless side of the access point to be in the same broadcast domain. Most firmware-based access points work this way and provide flexibility in your network configuration. You must compile bridging support into your kernel by adding the following line to your global configuration file:

```
pseudo-device    bridge    2      #network bridging support
```

The number following the bridge device indicates the number of possible bridges the host will be able to configure. For a standard configuration, two bridge devices should be fine. For larger or more complex installations, you may require more.

Once your kernel is configured properly, there are several different ways you can configure *HostAP* mode. The *wicontrol* utility provides a robust and complete interface to the configuration of the access point. The *ifconfig* utility, while slightly less functional, provides unified control of both layer 2 and layer 3 configuration parameters.

The *wicontrol* utility takes the following parameters for *HostAP* mode:

interface
> This specifies the interface *wicontrol* is to act on. If no interface is specified, *wicontrol* will configure the wi0 interface.

-p *port type*

This parameter specifies the mode of network to join or create. To activate *HostAP* mode on your card, use port type 6. The word hostap can be used interchangeably with 6 to make the command more readable.

-n *network name*

This is the SSID your access point will be configured with. This is the SSID string stations must use to connect to your access point.

-k *key [-v 1|2|3|4]*

This parameter controls the various WEP key used by stations to authenticate and encrypt traffic to your access point. key can be entered either as decimal (e.g., secrt) or as hexadecimal (e.g., 0x0123456789). The numbers following the key indicate which key index the specified key should be placed in. The WEP specification allows for four different keys to be stored for use in various key rotation strategies. If the –v flag is not specified, the first index is assumed.

-e *0|1*

Your access point can force stations to use WEP for authentication and data integrity by setting the -e flag to 1. If this parameter is set to 0, WEP is not required.

This is not a complete list of all of the commands *wicontrol* understands in *HostAP* mode. For a complete description, see the *wicontrol* manual page.

If you prefer the unified interface of *ifconfig*, the following parameters are relevant to *HostAP* mode:

interface

This is the interface *ifconfig* will operate on. The first Prism-based interface in the machine is known as wi0.

nwid *ssid*

This is the name of the service set to create. The value specified here is the SSID stations will use to connect to your access point.

nwkey *key*

This is the WEP key the access point will use to encrypt traffic to associated stations. key can be entered either as decimal (e.g., secrt) or as hexadecimal (e.g., 0x0123456789). If this value is not specified, the access point will not allow WEP connections.

mediaopt *hostap*

This parameter causes the card to enter access-point mode.

As of OpenBSD 3.1, *ifconfig* has limited wireless functionality. In order to make use of more advanced features such as WEP key rotation, power savings, and channel allocation, you must use *wicontrol*.

OpenBSD Startup Files

Configuring the access point by hand after each boot is unlikely to be your preferred administration mechanism. There are several startup files you can modify to start *HostAP* mode at boot time and bridge your wired and wireless interfaces together.

OpenBSD makes use of */etc/hostname.<interface>* files to configure each interface in the box. These files contain specific information regarding the interface's configuration as well as any arbitrary commands you wish to execute when the interface is brought online. For a complete discussion of the structure of these files, see the *hostname.if* manual page.

First, bring the wireless interface up in *HostAP* mode. Do not assign an IP address to the wireless interface. For this example, we are configuring an access point to run on channel 6 with an SSID of Example:

```
# /etc/hostname.wi0
up nwid Example mediaopt hostap
!wicontrol \$if -f 6
```

Next, bring up the wired interface on sis0. We will assign an IP to this interface and setup a default route. Note that for the IP address we must specify the IP address, the netmask, and the broadcast address:

```
# /etc/hostname.sis0
inet 192.168.0.2 255.255.255.0 192.168.0.255
!route add default 192.168.0.1
```

Finally, we must bring up the bridge interface. Like individual interfaces, bridges are controlled through files in */etc*. The first bridge group is identified as *bridgename.bridge0*, the second is *bridgename.bridge1*, etc. The *hostname.if* manual page also contains information on the bridgename files. In order for the bridge to function, we must add both the wired and wireless interfaces and then bring the bridge group up. The following lines are passed to *brconfig* at boot time:

```
# /etc/bridgename.bridge0
add wi0
add sis0
up
```

Reboot your machine, and you should have a bridging access point. If the access point does not work as expected, examine your log files.

Securing an OpenBSD Access Point

Now that you have a functioning access point, you should take steps to secure the access point and the network itself. By using the packet filtering firewall that comes with OpenBSD and MAC address filtering in the bridge interface, you can restrict access to your network and network devices.

A bridge is designed to allow all traffic between the bridged interfaces. The packet filtering firewall can sit in between the interfaces and remove hostile traffic. You may or may not decide to have the access point enforce a network security policy, but at the very least you should configure your firewall to protect the IP address of the access point itself. The following configuration file will allow all traffic through the access point but restrict access to the access point itself to SSH connections from a trusted host on the wired network:

```
# Simple access point pf.conf
# Wireless interface
oif = "wi0"
# Wired interface
eif = "sis0"
enet = "192.168.0.0"
emask = "255.255.255.0"
eip = "192.168.0.2"
# allow by default because this is a bridge
pass in all
pass out all
# allow localhost traffic
pass in quick on lo0 all
pass out quick on lo0 all
# protect self
block in inet from any to $eip
# pass ssh traffic for management from a trusted host that arrives on the
# wired network
pass in quick on $eif inet proto tcp from 192.168.0.11 to $eip port = 22 flags S/SA
keep state
```

Allowing management of the access point from the wireless network can be very dangerous. If possible, limit the management functions to the wired network.

You can also limit the MAC addresses allowed to communicate on the network. This is useful for attempting to control rogue wireless clients and rogue wired gateways. The *brconfig* utility provides functionality to control which MAC addresses can communicate across member interfaces in the bridge group. In a standard network, the gateway will be the only MAC address on the wired side. That should be the only source MAC address in packets received on the wired interface. Ideally, you will also know the MAC addresses of the stations on your wireless network so it can filter on source MAC addresses on the wireless interface.

The following is a *bridgename.bridge0* file that filters gateway and station MAC addresses:

```
# /etc/bridgename.bridge0
# Gateway has MAC address of 1:1:1:1:1:1
# clients have MAC addresses of 2:2:2:2:2:1 and 2:2:2:2:2:2
add sis0
add wi0
```

```
up
# allow gateway traffic in on wired network
rule pass in on sis0 src 1:1:1:1:1:1
# allow station traffic in on wireless network
rule pass in on wi0 src 2:2:2:2:2:1
rule pass in on wi0 src 2:2:2:2:2:2
# block everything else
rule block in on sis0
rule block in on wi0
```

If you prefer not to list all of the MAC filtering rules in the *bridgename.bridge0* file, you can create a separate file with the *ruleset* and use *brconfig* to process it. The following file will enforce the same policy as listed in the previous *bridgename.bridge0*. The file can be saved to any convenient location:

```
# Example /etc/bridge.rules
in on sis0 src 1:1:1:1:1:1
pass in on wi0 src 2:2:2:2:2:1
pass in on wi0 src 2:2:2:2:2:2
block in on sis0
block in on wi0
```

Use *brconfig* to load the *ruleset* for the *bridge0* interface by issuing the following command:

```
# brconfig bridge0 rulefile testbridge
```

Taking It to the Gateway

There is no guaranteed way to secure communications on an access point. However, there are many techniques you can employ to make your access point a difficult target. Firmware-based APs are easy to setup but provide limited usability and security options. The flexibility gained by deploying a Linux, FreeBSD, or OpenBSD access point is somewhat offset by the more technical configuration and security requirements of a general purpose OS. Whatever option you choose, raising the bar as high as possible is very important. Now that you understand how to properly configure an access point for secure use, it is time to move farther out into the network and examine the security on the gateway.

## PART IV

Gateway Security

Properly configured access points and clients are useless without a secure connection to other networks. Whether your gateway connects you to your intranet or proves transit to the greater Internet, it is the keystone of your security architecture. It is a central point for traffic to transfer through on its way to other networks. It is an excellent place to enforce a single security policy. Unfortunately, many networks do not make proper use of this keystone. Either through misconfiguration, or a complete lack of firewalling capability, networks around the world are wide open to attack. When the gateway is connected to a wireless network, the risk increases. Attackers are now on the doorstep of your valuable resources, and the role of the gateway becomes more important. The next four chapters will show you how to architect and configure a gateway that protects your wired and wireless resources.

## CHAPTER 10

Gateway Security

Until very recently, a firewall has been the frontline security device in most networks. Attacks have historically been launched against layer 3 or above. Firewalls have advanced over the years, evolving from glorified IP access lists to stateful, application aware security devices. With the wide-scale deployment of wireless networks, suddenly layer 1 and layer 2 security has become a hot topic. A wireless access point and wireless client must be able to defend themselves and their resources in an attempt to retain the integrity of the network.

This does not mean that firewalls have become less important in the bounds of a wireless network. Quite the contrary, a firewall, serving as a layer 3 gateway, is a critical piece of a wireless network. Not only must it defend against conventional attacks over the Internet, it must also protect itself and the networks it controls from unauthorized access originating from a hostile wireless network. A gateway is the first line of defense from an attacker who has complete physical and logical access.

Gateway Architecture

The first thing to consider when deploying a gateway that will face a wireless network is how it will fit into your overall network architecture. It is tempting to simply plug an access point into an existing wired network and use your existing firewall to secure it. This is a recipe for trouble. By placing your access point in the same broadcast domain as your other critical services, you give an attacker a direct connection to any machine on the wired network. Figure 10-1 shows an insecure placement of a bridging access point. The attacker is behind your firewall. Unless your access point is acting as a transparent firewall between the wired and wireless segments, enforcing access control becomes a difficult proposition.

Even with host-based access control on all hosts on the wired network, an attacker can still launch an ARP spoofing attack against the network. For a complete discussion of ARP spoofing, see "ARP Poisoning" in Chapter 2. An attacker, in an ARP spoofing attack, can serve as a man in the middle between two wired hosts. He can

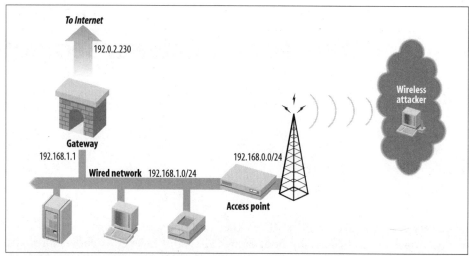

Figure 10-1. Insecure placement of access point

effectively pull packets off the wired network and force them to go across the wireless network.

To provide access control and minimize the risks of layer 2 attacks, the access point should be connected to its own interface on the gateway. Figure 10-2 shows the preferred architecture for a wireless network to be attached to a gateway. The figure also shows the corresponding IP address used in the examples in the chapters that follow.

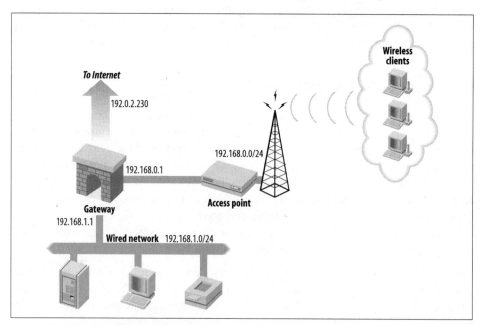

Figure 10-2. Proper architecture for single AP networks

Some networks may require multiple access points to cover the desired area. Ideally, all of the access points will be in the same service set and be located on the same subnet so users have transparent roaming capability. To provide a single point of security policy enforcement yet still allow roaming, your gateway should act as a transparent bridging firewall between the multiple interfaces servicing the wireless interfaces. Figure 10-3 shows an example of a bridging firewall connected to multiple networks in the same service set. In general, there is no reason for hosts associated to different access points to talk to each other. There will be no service offered from the workstations attached to the wireless network, so traffic between workstations may be an attack. A bridging firewall gives you the capability to limit interstation traffic.

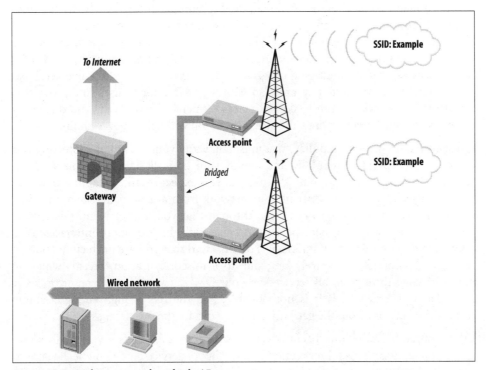

Figure 10-3. Architecture with multiple APs

Secure Installation

Regardless of the operating system you choose for your gateway, be sure it is installed in a secure manner. Completely disconnect the host from the network and use installation media that you trust. Vendors have different ways to verify their installation media. If you have downloaded an ISO CD image from an FTP server, there should be a checksum file with the ISO image that will allow you to verify the integrity of the data.

Once the operating system is installed, it is imperative that you check with your vendor for security patches. No matter how bug free an operating system was thought to be when it was released, security vulnerabilities will be found and used to create exploits over time. Before connecting your host to the network, download security patches from your vendor, copy them onto a trusted media, and install the patches from that media. This will allow you to have a high degree of assurance in your installation once you place it into production.

Firewall Rule Creation

Creating firewall rules for a network can be a painful process. The ruleset must be secure enough to only allow access to required resources. Unfortunately, what you as a security administrator think is a required resource and what the users of the network feel is a required resource can differ wildly. For example, many users believe instant-messenger programs are required for day-to-day communications and business processes. Instant-messaging programs may be great enablers of enhanced business communication, but they are also a prime vector for viruses and worms to invade your network. You must come to an agreement with the users and owners of the network when creating firewall rules, or else you will fight a never-ending battle.

Once everyone agrees on a policy, you must still verify your firewall is protecting you as you expect. Build your ruleset and deploy your firewall. Then examine your log files and verify you are dropping the packets you expect to and accepting the valid packets. It is advisable to portscan your network from a host facing each interface. Make sure you are not allowing traffic through that you do not want. Given how complicated a ruleset can become on a firewall with three or more interfaces, take your time and examine each interface. You may find that you are protecting yourself from wireless attacks effectively but, due to a misconfiguration, are allowing the entire Internet through to all services on your DMZ. If you discover an error, fix it immediately if possible. If it is not possible, and the risk is high enough, simply unplug the network from the gateway until you can fix the problem.

Open source firewalls have become very advanced in the last few years. Most firewalls now perform stateful inspection and quality of service enforcement. Be sure to read the documentation that comes with your firewall to get the latest information on cutting-edge features and possibilities.

Audit Logging

Your work as a security administrator is not over once the gateway is deployed and firewall rules are configured. A machine or network can be compromised at any time. You must be diligent in monitoring and upgrading your gateway to make sure it remains intact. The chapters that follow provide specific examples of auditing mechanisms you can use on your gateway. These examples are by no means the only options available to you for auditing and monitoring. There are many tools, free or otherwise, available to keep track of your gateway. Examine your needs, examine your options, and deploy what works for you. Regardless of what tools you use, be sure to use something. Complacency in monitoring your gateway will lead to a compromise down the road.

Deploying a gateway can be difficult. Configuration can be a complicated process, and understanding all the options presented to you can be dizzying. Try to keep your eye on the goal: keeping your network and services secure from attackers. If you find you are getting tired or confused, take a break and step back from the project. Your gateway is the keystone of your security architecture. Deploy it with all of the diligence it deserves.

CHAPTER 11

Building a Linux Gateway

So far, we have examined how to set up wireless clients and access points. We have examined how to use the clients and access points to secure the wireless network. The key piece that brings all of this together is the gateway. The gateway will connect the wireless network and any local wired connections to the Internet itself. Because of its role as the central connecting piece of the network, the gateway is also an ideal place to provide more layers of protection: separating the wired and wireless networks from each other and, from the most persistent source of attacks, the Internet.

 It is safest to configure and secure the gateway completely before ever connecting it to the Internet. Perform the initial install from a CD, and secure the box before connecting. If you connect a freshly installed, insecure computer to the Internet, there is a good chance it will be hacked before you have it fully set up. The current record for time from connection to completely hacked (to our knowledge) is 17 seconds.

Laying Out the Network

The gateway will have three network connections. The first is a connection to an ISP providing access to the Internet. This could take the form of a dialup, DSL, a cable modem, or higher bandwidth forms of access. In this chapter, we will approach it as an Ethernet card communicating with an external device that handles the connection. (This is commonly how DSL and cable modems work.) Throughout the examples, the Ethernet card connecting to this upstream provider will be referred to as the Linux network interface eth0.

A second Ethernet card will be used to connect to a switch or hub handling local wired connections. This is very useful for connecting local servers or desktop machines that don't have a wireless card. This network interface will be referred to as eth1.

There are two options for connecting the gateway to the wireless network. Another Ethernet interface can be used to connect to an external, stand-alone AP. Alternatively, the gateway can use a *HostAP* interface as described in Chapter 9. For simplicity, we will refer to this interface as eth2, as it would be in the case of an external AP. Remember that it could be setup either of these ways, but it won't affect the configuration as we discuss it in this chapter. (The network interface will be named wlan0 if *HostAP* is used.)

 Our gateway is going to provide services such as DHCP and NAT. If the external access point being used can also provide these services, make sure to disable them on the access point to prevent conflicts.

The role of the gateway is not very computationally demanding, so a fast computer is not a necessity. In a home network, an old Pentium computer with 64 MB of RAM would be able to fulfill this role quite nicely. The gateway does need to have three Ethernet network interfaces or two Ethernet interfaces and a wireless interface.

The duties of the gateway will encompass:

- Providing a firewall to protect both the internal networks—both from the Internet and from each other
- Providing NAT for both the internal networks
- Providing DHCP to allow for auto-configuring clients on the internal networks
- Optionally: providing a caching DNS server

All of these services can be handled under both Linux and FreeBSD. This chapter will cover how to set up the gateway using Linux. Chapter 12 will cover FreeBSD.

The actual IP addresses assigned to the interfaces connecting to the upstream provider and DNS services will vary from one ISP to the next. So in our examples, the following IP addresses will be used throughout this chapter:

- IP address assigned by ISP: 192.0.2.230 (assuming the ISP does not issue addresses using DHCP)
- DNS server run by ISP: 192.0.2.3

The DHCP server will be configured to assign IP addresses to wireless clients in the range 192.168.0.100 to 192.168.0.200 and to wired clients in the range 192.168.1.100 to 192.168.1.200, as shown in Figure 11-1.

Building the Gateway

Once the gateway hardware has been assembled, it is time to install the operating system and configure it to provide the necessary services. The installation should be as minimal as possible. Any unnecessary services and programs that are installed

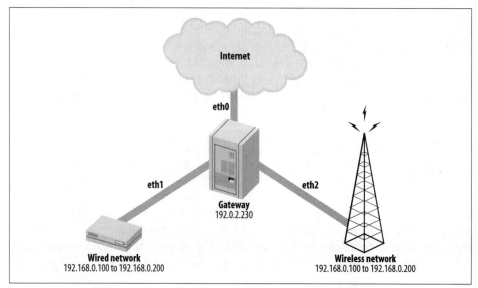

Figure 11-1. Example network

only increase the risk that one of the programs on the gateway may be vulnerable. Do not install the X Windows System or any of the optional applications.

It is important to install the development tools and the system source code. After installation, the kernel will be recompiled and the new versions of several services might need to be downloaded and compiled, so the development tools will be necessary.

Make the */var* partition of decent size during the drive setup. A couple hundred megabytes should be more than sufficient. A gateway can generate many logs, and this is where they will be stored.

If the installer for the distribution you are using has a firewall-configuration section (like the current RedHat installers), leave it unchanged for now. The firewall rules will be changed once the system is running and will be more complex than the basic configuration tool in the installer can generate.

Linux Kernel Configuration

The kernel configuration should be reviewed to remove unneeded support. Take out support for anything that won't be needed for the hardware configuration of the gateway. The general process for doing this is described in Chapter 5 (see "Kernel Configuration" and especially "Security Kernel Configuration"). Enable the optional modules for *Netfilter*; the firewall on the gateway will use several of these modules. The gateway will also need support for SYN cookies and IP forwarding.

If the gateway is going to connect to the wireless network using *HostAP* or a wireless network card instead of an Ethernet connection to the AP, make sure the kernel has support for the wireless drivers selected.

Disabling Unneeded Services

Just as with the clients, the unneeded services on the gateway should be disabled. The basic approach to doing this for Linux is described in Chapter 5.

Check to see what services are running and disable all of the unneeded remotely accessible services. Don't forget to check the *inetd* or *xinetd* services as well as the *rc*-based services.

The services that will be used, and should be enabled, are *arpwatch*, *syslog*, *dhcpd*, and *sshd*. *arpwatch* and *syslog* will be used for monitoring and logging. *dhcpd* will provide DHCP addresses to clients. To allow remote administration of the gateway *sshd* must be running. This will provide encrypted shell sessions from the *ssh* client program.

Disable the *iptables* and *ipchains* services in *rc*; a replacement script will be developed later in this chapter to configure the *iptables* service.

Configuring Network Interfaces

The three network interfaces need to be configured with the proper settings for the network layout we are putting together.

The file */etc/sysconfig/network-scripts/ifcfg-eth0* will contain the settings for eth0. If your ISP provides IP addresses by DHCP, the file should contain:

```
DEVICE=eth0
ONBOOT=yes
BOOTPROTO=DHCP
```

Otherwise, it should contain the following:

```
DEVICE=eth0
ONBOOT=yes
BOOTPROTO=none
BROADCAST=192.0.2.255
NETWORK=192.0.2.0
NETMASK=255.255.255.0
IPADDR=192.0.2.230
GATEWAY=192.0.2.1
USERCTL=no
```

Replace NETWORK, BROADCAST, IPADDR, and GATEWAY with the proper values assigned to you by the ISP.

The file */etc/sysconfig/network-scripts/ifcfg-eth1* will contain the settings for the interface connected to the wired network:

```
DEVICE=eth1
BOOTPROTO=none
ONBOOT=yes
BROADCAST=192.168.1.255
NETWORK=192.168.1.0
NETMASK=255.255.255.0
IPADDR=192.168.1.1
USERCTL=no
```

This will set eth1 to have the IP address 192.168.1.1 and be connected to the network 192.168.1.0/24.

If the wireless network is going to be provided by using *HostAP* on the gateway itself, set up that interface as described in Chapter 9. Otherwise, eth2 will be connected to the access point and will be configured in */etc/sysconfig/network-scripts/ifcfg-eth1*:

```
DEVICE=eth2
BOOTPROTO=none
ONBOOT=yes
BROADCAST=192.168.0.255
NETWORK=192.168.0.0
NETMASK=255.255.255.0
IPADDR=192.168.0.1
USERCTL=no
```

This will set eth2 to have the IP address 192.168.0.1 and be connected to the network 192.168.0.0/24.

Building the Firewall Rules

The most important responsibility of the gateway is to firewall our three separate network segments. We will again use the *Netfilter* functionality that was introduced in "Firewall Configuration" in Chapter 5. See that section for a basic introduction to the functioning of *Netfilter*.

The *rc.firewall* script for the gateway is significantly more complex that the one laid out for use on the clients. It has to protect not only the gateway itself, but also ensure separation between the networks while allowing vital services on the gateway to be accessed by local users. This script is also much more aggressive in preventing abusive behavior since it will be the frontline against often hazardous Internet traffic.

This script is quite long; we will examine it section by section. To build the completed script, concatenate each of the example sections that follow into */etc/init.d/rc.firewall*.

First, we establish several variables that will be used throughout the rest of the script. By placing these values into variables, we can easily update the script if these values change in the future. Here we define the three network interfaces that will be used

for the upstream, wired, and wireless connections, respectively. Change these to
match the configuration of your machine.

```
#!/bin/sh
# rc.firewall for gateway

# --- SETUP ---

# Variables (for easier changes)
IPTABLES=/sbin/iptables

INT_GW="eth0"
INT_WIRED="eth1"
INT_WIRELESS="eth2"
INT_ALL="$INT_GW $INT_WIRED $INT_WIRELESS lo"
```

The IP_ variables hold the IP addresses or ranges that will be used in the firewall
rules. IP_GW is the address of the upstream connection interface. If your ISP assigns
addresses using DHCP instead of static IP addresses, use the commented-out example, which will extract the DHCP-assigned address from *ifconfig*. (Note the command is enclosed in backticks, not quotes.) IP_WIRED holds the address range for our
internal wired network, and IP_WIRELESS holds the address range for the internal
wireless network. IP_GW_WIRED and IP_GW_WIRELESS hold the respective IP addresses
for the network interfaces on the gateway that are connected to those networks.
Change these to match the configuration of your networks and your ISP's network.

```
# For DHCP use: IP_GW=`/sbin/ifconfig $INT_GW | grep inet | cut -f2 -d: | cut -f1 -d\ `
IP_GW="192.0.2.230"
IP_WIRED="192.168.1.0/24"
IP_WIRELESS="192.168.0.0/24"
IP_GW_WIRED="192.168.1.1"
IP_GW_WIRELESS="192.168.0.1"xxxxxxx
```

The next section in the script sets a number of values in the */proc* file system. These
settings should help to reduce certain types of malicious behavior directed at the network and the gateway. The comments in this snippet of the script provide a brief
description of what each setting does.

```
# /proc variables

# Ignore broadcast pings
echo "1" > /proc/sys/net/ipv4/icmp_echo_ignore_broadcasts
# Ignore bogus ICMP errors
echo "1" > /proc/sys/net/ipv4/icmp_ignore_bogus_error_responses
# Limit the reply rate to pings
echo "100" > /proc/sys/net/ipv4/icmp_echoreply_rate
# Use TCP SYN cookies
echo "1" > /proc/sys/net/ipv4/tcp_syncookies

# Do the following for each interface being used
```

```
for INT in $INT_ALL; do
    # Disable acceptance of redirects
    echo "0" > /proc/sys/net/ipv4/conf/$INT/accept_redirects
    # Disable source routing
    echo "0" > /proc/sys/net/ipv4/conf/$INT/accept_source_route
    # Enable routing verification to prevent spoofing of invalid IPs
    echo "1" > /proc/sys/net/ipv4/conf/$INT/rp_filter
    # Disable bootp relaying
    echo "0" > /proc/sys/net/ipv4/conf/$INT/bootp_relay
done
```

At this point, calls to *iptables* begin to set up the firewall ruleset. First, all of the existing rules are flushed. Then a default policy is set up which will drop all traffic sent to the gateway and forward it to other networks. Traffic from the gateway will be allowed by default.

```
# --- BEGIN IPTABLES SETTINGS ---

# Flush all chains to get a clean start
$IPTABLES -F
$IPTABLES -X
$IPTABLES -t nat -F

# Set default policies
$IPTABLES -P INPUT DROP
$IPTABLES -P OUTPUT ACCEPT
$IPTABLES -P FORWARD DROP
```

An exception is then made to allow the gateway to communicate unrestricted over the local loopback interface.

```
# Allow local loopback traffic
$IPTABLES -A INPUT -i lo -j ACCEPT
$IPTABLES -A OUTPUT -o lo -j ACCEPT
```

These two commands establish chains of rules called allowed_icmp, to_gateway, and forward_checks. These chains will be used to consolidate sets of rules that will be used in multiple places.

```
# Create chains for common series of rules
$IPTABLES -N allowed_icmp
$IPTABLES -N to_gateway
$IPTABLES -N forward_checks
```

The next large block of the script will establish the rules to filter traffic being forwarded between any of the three interfaces in the gateway. This traffic will have to pass the rules defined for the FORWARD chain.

```
# --- FORWARDING ---
$IPTABLES -A FORWARD -j forward_checks
# Drop everything else.  This includes traffic between wired and wireless networks!
$IPTABLES -A FORWARD -j LOG
$IPTABLES -A FORWARD -j DROP
```

We tell the actual FORWARD chain to use the forward_checks chain that follows. To finish the FORWORD rules off, we log and drop any packets that were not accepted by one of the preceding forwarding rules.

```
# Allow established connections to come from Internet to wired and wireless networks
$IPTABLES -A forward_checks -m state --state ESTABLISHED,RELATED -j ACCEPT
```

This rule uses the state tracking abilities of *Netfilter* to allow any packets that are part of an existing and already approved connection to be forwarded.

```
# Allow wired and wireless networks to establish new connections
#  Check for proper source addresses for each source interface
$IPTABLES -A forward_checks -m state --state NEW -s $IP_WIRED -i $INT_WIRED -o $INT_
GW -j ACCEPT
$IPTABLES -A forward_checks -m state --state NEW -s $IP_WIRELESS -i $INT_WIRELESS -o
$INT_GW -j ACCEPT
```

Using the state tracking facilities again, these two rules allow new connections to be started. Note the rules use –s to check the source IP addresses, -i to check the source interface, and –o to check the destination interface. This will ensure that clients on the wired and wireless networks can only create connections if they are using an IP address in the proper range for that network. Because –o specifies $INT_GW in both rules, connections can only be created to destinations that will routed through the upstream interface. These two rules will not allow connections to be created that connect between the wired and wireless networks.

```
# Allow certain ICMP packets
$IPTABLES -A forward_checks -p icmp -j allowed_icmp
```

This rule uses the allowed_icmp chain to examine any ICMP packets that are being forwarded. The rules for this chain are defined later in the script.

```
# Reject ident requests
$IPTABLES -A forward_checks -p tcp --dport 113 -j REJECT
```

Some daemons, namely *sendmail*, will query *ident* on hosts that attempt to use their service. By rejecting these requests rather than dropping them silently, the daemons will not have to wait for the *ident* query to timeout. This speeds up connections to these daemons, such as sending mail.

Another set of rules has to be constructed to filter the traffic destined for the gateway itself. The INPUT chain holds the rules that filter this traffic.

```
# -- CONNECTIONS TO/FROM THE GATEWAY ---

# Examine traffic from all three interfaces to gateway using same chain of rules
$IPTABLES -A INPUT -d $IP_GW -j to_gateway
$IPTABLES -A INPUT -d $IP_WIRED -j to_gateway
$IPTABLES -A INPUT -d $IP_WIRELESS -j to_gateway
$IPTABLES -A INPUT -j LOG
$IPTABLES -A INPUT -j DROP
```

Since there are three interfaces on the gateway, and we want to apply similar rules to all three interfaces, traffic destined for the three interfaces is all sent to the to_gateway chain. Any other traffic that happens to somehow end up in the INPUT chain is logged and dropped.

The to_gateway chain will prevent improper connections to the gateway itself and open up access to the services that we want to provide from the gateway.

```
# Allow all established traffic
$IPTABLES -A to_gateway -i $INT_GW -d $IP_GW -m state --state ESTABLISHED,RELATED -j
ACCEPT
$IPTABLES -A to_gateway -i $INT_WIRED -d $IP_GW_WIRED -m state --state
ESTABLISHED,RELATED -j ACCEPT
$IPTABLES -A to_gateway -i $INT_WIRELESS -d $IP_GW_WIRELESS -m state --state
ESTABLISHED,RELATED -j ACCEPT
```

These three rules accept traffic from established connections on the three interfaces. The checking of the input interface in the three rules is to ensure that clients can only communicate with the correct one of the gateway IPs for the segment of the network on which they are located.

```
# Allow ssh from anywhere to all the gateway IP addresses
$IPTABLES -A to_gateway -p tcp -i $INT_GW -d $IP_GW --dport 22 -j ACCEPT
$IPTABLES -A to_gateway -p tcp -i $INT_GW_WIRED -d $IP_GW_WIRED --dport 22 -j ACCEPT
$IPTABLES -A to_gateway -p tcp -i $INT_GW_WIRELESS -d $IP_GW_WIRELESS --dport 22 -j
ACCEPT
```

To provide access to the SSH server on the gateway, we allow clients on any of the three interfaces to connect to port 22 on the proper gateway IP address.

```
# Allow DHCP connections from wired and wireless networks
$IPTABLES -A to_gateway -p udp -i $INT_WIRED --dport 68 -j ACCEPT
$IPTABLES -A to_gateway -p udp -i $INT_WIRELESS --dport 68 -j ACCEPT
```

DHCP connections are sent to port 68 of 255.255.255.255. Because of this, we don't want to filter on the destination IP. They originate from 0.0.0.0, since the client doesn't have an address yet so we don't want to filter on the source address either. These two rules just check that the DHCP request came from either the wired or wireless network; we definitely don't want to answer DHCP requests on the ISP's network.

```
# Allow wired and wireless networks to connect to DNS
$IPTABLES -A to_gateway -p udp -i $INT_WIRED -s $IP_WIRED -d $IP_GW_WIRED --dport 53
-j ACCEPT
$IPTABLES -A to_gateway -p udp -i $INT_WIRELESS -s $IP_WIRELESS -d $IP_GW_WIRELESS --
dport 53 -j ACCEPT
```

These rules are only necessary if you want to run a local DNS server. Our DNS server is only going to act as a cache for the local clients and will serve them on UDP port 53. It only needs to accept connections from the local networks, so we perform the standard checks for appropriate source interface, source IP address, and destination IP address.

```
# Filter inbound ICMP
$IPTABLES -A to_gateway -p icmp -j allowed_icmp
```

Just like the in the FORWARD chain, ICMP packets will be filtered using the allowed_icmp chain.

```
# Reject ident requests
$IPTABLES -A to_gateway -p tcp --dport 113 -j REJECT
```

Again, like the FORWARD chain, this will speed up *sendmail* connections.

```
# Drop everything else
$IPTABLES -A to_gateway -j LOG
$IPTABLES -A to_gateway -j DROP
```

Anything that hasn't been accepted by the to_gateway rules should be logged and dropped.

```
# Let the gateway connect to anywhere
$IPTABLES -A OUTPUT -j ACCEPT
```

The OUTPUT chain will simply allow the gateway to connect to anything it wants. You can definitely make this more restrictive if you want to limit where the gateway can connect to.

```
# --- COMMON ICMP RULE CHAIN ---

# Allow certain ICMP messages
$IPTABLES -A allowed_icmp -p icmp --icmp-type pong -j ACCEPT
$IPTABLES -A allowed_icmp -p icmp --icmp-type source-quench -j ACCEPT
$IPTABLES -A allowed_icmp -p icmp --icmp-type time-exceeded -j ACCEPT
$IPTABLES -A allowed_icmp -p icmp --icmp-type destination-unreachable -j ACCEPT
$IPTABLES -A allowed_icmp -p icmp --icmp-type parameter-problem -j ACCEPT
```

This defines the rules for the allowed_icmp chain that is used by both FORWARD and INPUT. It allows management packets such as answers to pings, source quench, time exceeded, destination unreachable, and parameter problem messages. Blocking these particular ICMP messages can cause excessive waits for time outs on the clients when something goes wrong with a connection. Most of the other ICMP messages are unneeded normally; some, like redirects, can be downright dangerous.

```
# --- NAT ---

# Perform NAT masquerading for traffic bound to Internet
# For DHCP use: $IPTABLES -t nat -A POSTROUTING -o $INT_GW -j MASQUERADE
$IPTABLES -t nat -A POSTROUTING -o $INT_GW -j SNAT --to $IP_GW
```

This rule provides source network address translation for all traffic heading out of the gateway upstream interface. It uses a special chain called POSTROUTING that processes the packets after the FORWARD and OUTPUT chains. All the packets from the gateway and both internal networks will be mapped to the gateways external address before being sent. If the external address of the gateway is set by DHCP, you should use the alternate NAT rule in the comment instead. The MASQUERADE-style NAT handles changes in IP addresses more gracefully and resets its state tables to prevent the packet mangling that can occur if the address changes while connections are active.

```
# -- TURN ON FORWARDING ---

# Enable IP forwarding
echo 1 > /proc/sys/net/ipv4/ip_forward
```

The script concludes with one last setting to a */proc* file, which will enable the routing of IP packets between the interfaces in the gateway.

That's it! Place the completed script in */etc/init.d/rc.firewall*, mark it as executable using *chmod*, and call it from the *rc.local* file. It will then be called when the system starts up.

 If you find after a while that all the spurious traffic with spoofed source IP addresses is filling up your logs, consider removing the log command from some of the rules in this ruleset.

There are several good references on building *Netfilter* rulesets at *http://www. netfilter.org* and *http://www.linuxsecurity.com/resources/firewalls-1.html*. There are also many people who have posted example firewall scripts on web sites for people to look at; search around and look at them for alternate ways to build your rulesets, and additional protections to set up.

MAC Address Filtering

One way of limiting which wireless clients can successfully communicate is to limit traffic based on the MAC address of the wireless cards. First, create a chain to hold the MAC filtering rules (place this with the other chain creation commands):

```
$IPTABLES -N mac_filter
```

Create a section in the rule file to hold the MAC address related rules. For each MAC you want to be allowed to send traffic from the wireless network, add a rule of the following syntax:

```
$IPTABLES -A mac_filter -i $INT_WIRELESS -m mac --mac-source 01:01:01:01:01:01  -j
forward_checks
```

After all of those rules have been created, three last rules are needed to block everything else that is coming from the wireless network:

```
$IPTABLES -A mac_filter -i ! $INT_WIRELESS -j ACCEPT
$IPTABLES -A mac_filter -j LOG
$IPTABLES -A mac_filter -j DROP
```

To insert these MAC filtering rules into the forwarding system we need to replace the existing line:

```
$IPTABLES -A FORWARD -j forward_checks
```

with a line that jumps to the MAC filter chain:

```
$IPTABLES -A FORWARD -j mac_filter
```

The `mac_filter` chain will then jump to the `forward_checks` chain when a matching MAC is found.

Filtering based on MAC addresses is not a perfect security solution. It is very easy to change the MAC address of a wireless card. An attacker can snoop the traffic on the wireless network, learn what MAC addresses are being used successfully, and then change her card to use the discovered MAC. Maintaining the list of allowed MAC addresses for anything but a small network can quickly become overwhelming as well.

DHCP

The DHCP daemon will provide automatic assignment of IP addresses to hosts on the local wired and wireless networks. Make sure that the *dhcpd* service has been enabled in the *rc* files. If it is not installed on your system, you can get the latest version from *http://www.isc.org/products/DHCP/*.

The configuration of the DHCP daemon is stored in the file */etc/dhcpd.conf*. Edit this file to contain:

```
subnet 192.0.2.0 netmask 255.255.255.0 {
        not authoritative;
}

subnet 192.168.0.0 netmask 255.255.255.0 {
        option domain-name-servers 19.0.2.3;
        option routers 192.168.0.1;
        range 192.168.0.100 192.168.0.200;
}

subnet 192.168.1.0 netmask 255.255.255.0 {
        option domain-name-servers 192.0.2.3;
        option routers 192.168.1.1;
        range 192.168.1.100 192.168.1.200;
}
```

The three subnet clauses in this file correspond to the three interfaces on the gateway.

Ensure that the subnet address and net mask of the first clause match that of the interface connected to your upstream provider. The statement not authoritative tells the DHCP daemon not to assign DHCP addresses on that interface.

The other two clauses will be used to assign addresses to the clients on the 192.168. 0.0 and 192.168.1.0 networks. The option routers statement will tell the clients to use the IP address of the corresponding gateway interface as a router for outbound traffic. The option domain-name-servers statement tells the clients what DNS server to use. Change this to be the DNS server provided by your ISP. If you want to run a caching DNS server as described in the next section, change it to match the gateway address in the option routers statement.

DNS

In the DHCP configuration outlined in the previous section, the clients are sent the upstream providers DNS server IP addresses. This is the simplest way to set things up, but you might want to go to a step further and run your own DNS server.

There are two common reasons to run your own DNS server: caching DNS lookups for performance reasons or hosting a domain. DNS caching can improve performance by handling repeated DNS lookups locally. This probably won't make a very big difference unless your upstream DNS server has noticeable delays. The proper hosting of a domain is a more advanced topic; if you wish to do this, you should consult the DNS server documentation for information on configuration.

By running DNS as an additional service on the gateway, a new potential point of vulnerability is introduced. BIND, the most widely used DNS server, has a history of security issues. To help limit exposure, it should be set up in a *chroot* environment. The latest version of BIND and documentation can be found at *http://www.isc.org/products/BIND/*.

If you do decide to configure the gateway with a caching DNS server, make sure you change the DHCP configuration file to give the proper gateway IP addresses in option domain-name-server. The address will be different for the wired and wireless segments as the gateway's two interfaces for those segments have different IP addresses. The DNS server should also have zone files to handle reverse lookups on your internal address space by the clients.

Static ARP

ARP poisoning attacks, discussed in Chapter 2, are a real threat to all entities on a wireless network, including the gateway. An ARP attack against the gateway could cut off all network connectivity to the clients. The possibility of a successful ARP attack can be reduced by setting up static ARP entries for IP addresses that we know ahead of time.

In the case of the gateway, two particular IP addresses can benefit most from static ARP: the IP of the access point, and the IP of the cable modem or router.

Add two lines to the end of */etc/rc.local*:

```
arp -s <AP IP> <AP MAC>
arp -s <ROUTER IP> <ROUTER MAC>
```

If there are any hosts on the wired network that are going to act as servers and will not be using DHCP to get dynamic addresses, it wouldn't hurt to create static ARP entries for them too.

Audit Logging

Proper auditing is even more important on the gateway than it is on the client machines. The gateway is the contact point with the outside world, and it will receive nonstop abuse from all over the Internet. Because of this, it's vital to keep a good eye on the logs of this machine.

The services *arpwatch*, *syslog*, and *swatch* should all be installed and configured in the same fashion as described for the Linux client machines in Chapter 5.

Don't forget to periodically log in to the gateway and check the logs and root user mail for evidence of a security breach. Even better, forward this information to an email account you check often.

Wrapping Up

At this point, everything should be all set on the gateway. It's a good idea to reboot and make sure all the services start up without any errors. Fire up a wireless client, and check to make sure it gets an IP address and can access the Internet.

Make sure that you keep an eye on the security of the gateway. Periodically check for updated versions of the software running on the gateway, and subscribe to any security announcement email lists related to the distribution you are using. It's everyone's job to help keep the Internet secure; don't let your brand-new gateway become a springboard for someone to hack other computers.

## CHAPTER 12

Building a FreeBSD Gateway

The previous chapter examined building a Linux based gateway. Building a FreeBSD gateway for a wireless network is very similar. This chapter will examine the steps to set up a FreeBSD gateway comparable in function and behavior to the Linux gateway already described. The example network architecture we will be using in this chapter is the same as in the previous chapter.

Unlike with Linux, network interfaces have different names based on the type of hardware. Throughout this chapter, we will use dc0, dc1, and dc2 as the network interfaces. These correspond to the common *Netgear* and *Linksys* cards sold in most stores. Replace these with the names you have created for the three interfaces.

Building the Gateway

The first step is to install the operating system and configure it to provide the necessary services. The installation should be minimal as possible. Any unnecessary services and programs that are installed only increase the risk that one of the programs on the gateway may be vulnerable. Do not install the X Windows System or any of the optional applications.

It is important to install the development tools and the system source code. After installation, you will need to recompile the kernel and the new versions of several services might need to be downloaded and compiled, so the development tools will be necessary. The ports collection along with the *cvsup* utility will be helpful in installing and updating services too, so it might be a good idea to install those. Information on ports and *cvsup* can be found at *http://www.freebsd.org/doc/en_US. ISO8859-1/books/handbook/ports-using.html*.

Make the */var* partition of decent size during the drive setup. A couple hundred megabytes should be more than sufficient. A gateway can generate many logs and this is where they will be stored.

FreeBSD Kernel Configuration

The kernel configuration should be reviewed to remove unneeded support. Take out support for anything that won't be needed for the hardware configuration of the gateway. The general process for doing this and the details of options are described in Chapter 4 (see "Wireless Kernel Configuration" and especially "Security Kernel Configuration"). Enable the following options to add support for the firewall, NAT translation, randomizing IP identifiers, and dropping TCP SYN/FIN packets:

```
options IPFIREWALL
options IPFIREWALL_VERBOSE
options IPFIREWALL_VERBOSE_LIMIT=10
options IPDIVERT
options RANDOM_IP_ID
options TCP_DROP_SYNFIN
pseudo-device bpf
```

The only option here that we have not discussed yet is IPDIVERT, which enables support for divert rules in the firewall. Divert rules will be used to funnel packets to *natd*, the daemon which performs NAT translation on FreeBSD.

If the gateway is going to connect to the wireless network using *HostAP* or a wireless network card instead of an Ethernet connection to the AP, make sure the kernel has support for the wireless drivers selected and has the proper options set. The options are described in "Wireless Kernel Configuration" in Chapter 4 and the *HostAP* instructions of Chapter 9.

Disabling Unneeded Services

Just as with the clients, the unneeded services on the gateway should be disabled. The basic approach to doing this is described in Chapter 4. This machine should only have a minimal set of services running. An example */etc/rc.conf* appropriate for the gateway we are building should contain the following settings.

Set the upstream router this gateway will communicate with to 192.0.2.1.

```
defaultrouter="192.0.2.1"
```

Enable gateway behavior. This will cause packets to be forwarded between the interfaces. Then, set the hostname to "gateway".

```
gateway_enable="YES"
hostname="gateway"
```

This sets up the IP addresses and netmasks for the three network interfaces. There are no separate configuration files as there are under Linux. Change these to suit your network layout:

```
ifconfig_dc0="inet 192.0.2.230  netmask 255.255.255.0"
ifconfig_dc1="inet 192.168.0.1 netmask 255.255.255.0"
ifconfig_dc2="inet 192.168.1.1 netmask 255.255.255.0"
```

Setting the kernel security level to 3 prevents changing of certain settings without a reboot. One important thing this does is to prevent someone from changing the firewall rules while the system is running. You might want to set kern_securelevel_ enable to NO while you are getting things set up; it will save you a few reboots while you fine tune the firewall rules and other settings. Remember to come back and re-enable this when you are done building the gateway.

```
kern_securelevel="3"
kern_securelevel_enable="YES"
```

Disable NFS, sendmail, and *inetd*. We won't need these or any of the services that are started from *inetd*.

```
nfs_server_enable="NO"
sendmail_enable="NONE"
inetd_enable="NO"
```

To allow remote administration of the gateway *sshd* will need to be running. This will provide encrypted shell sessions from the ssh client program.

```
sshd_enable="YES"
```

Enable the firewall, and tell it to log results. The firewall type is set to "unknown" here, as we will be using a separate script to load the rules. Entering "unknown" will cause rc.firewall to set up basic firewall settings but not load rules.

```
firewall_enable="YES"
firewall_type="unknown"
firewall_logging="YES"
```

This enables the NAT daemon and tells it the outside interface is dc0. It will translate the addresses in packets only when they traverse this interface. Replace this with your external interface name.

```
natd_enable="YES"
natd_interface="dc0"
```

The last three settings drop and log ICMP redirect packets and drop TCP SYN/FIN packets. These types of packets should not be seen as part of normal traffic.

```
icmp_drop_redirect="YES"
icmp_log_redirect="YES"
tcp_drop_synfin="YES"
```

Building the Firewall Rules

The most important responsibility of the gateway is to firewall our three separate network segments. We will again use the *ipfw* functionality that was introduced in "Firewall configuration" in Chapter 4. See that section for a basic introduction to the functioning of *ipfw*.

The configuration script for the gateway is significantly more complex that the one laid out for use on the clients. It has to protect not only the gateway itself, but also ensure separation between the networks while allowing vital services on the gateway to be accessed by local users. This script is also much more aggressive in preventing abusive behavior since it will be the frontline against often hazardous Internet traffic.

We will examine the script section by section. To build the completed script, concatenate each of the example sections that follow into */etc/.firewall.conf.*

The first line sets the fwcmd variable equal to the path and name of the firewall control program.

```
fwcmd="/sbin/ipfw"
```

These four variables correspond to your outside interface, network, netmask, and IP address, respectively. Change these to the correct values.

```
# set these to your outside interface network and netmask and ip
oif="dc0"
onet="192.0.2.0"
omask="255.255.255.0"
oip="192.0.2.230"
```

These variables do the same thing for the wireless network (variables starting with "w") and for the internal wired network (variables starting with "i"). Change these if you are going to use different IP ranges on these networks.

```
# set these to your inside interface networks, netmasks, and IPs
wif="dc0"
wnet="192.168.0.0"
wmask="255.255.255.0"
wip="192.168.0.1"

iif="dc1"
inet="192.168.1.0"
imask="255.255.255.0"
iip="192.168.1.1"
```

These rules prevent traffic that appears to be from one of our three networks but actually originates on the wrong network. For example, a packet with the source IP of a wireless client should not come into the gateway from the wired network or the external network.

```
# Stop spoofing
${fwcmd} add deny all from ${inet}:${imask} to any in via ${oif}
${fwcmd} add deny all from ${wnet}:${wmask} to any in via ${oif}
${fwcmd} add deny all from ${onet}:${omask} to any in via ${iif}
${fwcmd} add deny all from ${onet}:${omask} to any in via ${wif}
${fwcmd} add deny all from ${inet}:${imask} to any in via ${wif}
${fwcmd} add deny all from ${wnet}:${wmask} to any in via ${iif}
```

These rules are the same as those found in the simple firewall section of the default */etc/rc.firewall*. They block incoming packets from the Internet destined to improper network IP ranges such as non-routable, multicast, and broadcast IPs.

```
# Stop RFC1918 nets on the outside interface
${fwcmd} add deny all from any to 10.0.0.0/8 via ${oif}
${fwcmd} add deny all from any to 172.16.0.0/12 via ${oif}
${fwcmd} add deny all from any to 192.168.0.0/16 via ${oif}

# Stop draft-manning-dsua-03.txt (1 May 2000) nets (includes RESERVED-1,
# DHCP auto-configuration, NET-TEST, MULTICAST (class D), and class E)
# on the outside interface
${fwcmd} add deny all from any to 0.0.0.0/8 via ${oif}
${fwcmd} add deny all from any to 169.254.0.0/16 via ${oif}
${fwcmd} add deny all from any to 192.0.2.0/24 via ${oif}
${fwcmd} add deny all from any to 224.0.0.0/4 via ${oif}
${fwcmd} add deny all from any to 240.0.0.0/4 via ${oif}
```

This rule tells the firewall that at this point in the processing, all packets that are being handled by the external interface should be sent to the NAT daemon for IP address translation.

```
${fwcmd} add divert natd all from any to any via ${oif}
```

Very similar in function to the block of rules above the NAT divert, these rules prevent packets originating from improper networks that come in from the external interface. This is done after the NAT translation so our internal network traffic is not inadvertently blocked by the RFC1918 filters.

```
# Stop RFC1918 nets on the outside interface
${fwcmd} add deny all from 10.0.0.0/8 to any via ${oif}
${fwcmd} add deny all from 172.16.0.0/12 to any via ${oif}
${fwcmd} add deny all from 192.168.0.0/16 to any via ${oif}

# Stop draft-manning-dsua-03.txt (1 May 2000) nets (includes RESERVED-1,
# DHCP auto-configuration, NET-TEST, MULTICAST (class D), and class E)
# on the outside interface
${fwcmd} add deny all from 0.0.0.0/8 to any via ${oif}
${fwcmd} add deny all from 169.254.0.0/16 to any via ${oif}
${fwcmd} add deny all from 192.0.2.0/24 to any via ${oif}
${fwcmd} add deny all from 224.0.0.0/4 to any via ${oif}
${fwcmd} add deny all from 240.0.0.0/4 to any via ${oif}
```

This rule allows packets that are part of an established TCP session to pass through the gateway.

```
# Allow TCP through if setup succeeded
${fwcmd} add pass tcp from any to any established
```

This allows UDP DNS traffic to and from a caching DNS server on the gateway. If you are not going to put a caching DNS server on the gateway, don't bother with these four rules.

```
# Allow access to our DNS
${fwcmd} add pass udp from any to ${wip} 53
${fwcmd} add pass udp from ${wip} 53 to any
${fwcmd} add pass udp from any to ${iip} 53
${fwcmd} add pass udp from ${iip} 53 to any
```

This rule allows the gateway itself to make DNS queries to the outside world. The keep-state directive tells it to expect a matching answer that should be passed through the firewall.

```
# Allow DNS queries out to the world
${fwcmd} add pass udp from ${oip} to any 53 keep-state
```

This rule allows connections to the SSH daemon from anywhere. This will allow secure connections to the gateway for administration from anywhere.

```
# Allow SSH connections
${fwcmd} add pass tcp from any to ${oip} 22
${fwcmd} add pass tcp from any to ${wip} 22
${fwcmd} add pass tcp from any to ${iip} 22
```

Some daemons, namely *sendmail*, will query *ident* on hosts that attempt to use their service. By rejecting these requests rather than dropping them silently, the daemons will not have to wait for the *ident* query to timeout. This speeds up connections to these daemons, such as sending mail.

```
${fwcmd} add reset tcp from any to any 113
```

Attempts to start new TCP connections originating from the Internet should be rejected and logged.

```
# Reject&Log all setup of incoming connections from the outside
${fwcmd} add deny log tcp from any to any in via ${oif} setup
```

These three rules allow TCP connections originating from the wireless network, wired network, or gateway to be made. The setup directive tells the firewall to add the connection to the state table so that packets in the session are passed by the pass … established rule above. Note that connections between the wired and wireless networks are not authorized by these rules.

```
# Allow setup of other TCP connections
${fwcmd} add pass tcp from ${wnet}:${wmask} to any out via ${oif} setup
${fwcmd} add pass tcp from ${inet}:${imask} to any out via ${oif} setup
${fwcmd} add pass tcp from ${oip} to any out via ${oif} setup
```

This allows ICMP echo reply, source quench, time exceeded, destination unreachable, and parameter problem messages to be passed.

```
# Allow ICMP
${fwcmd} add pass icmp from any to any icmptypes 0,3,4,11,12
```

Everything else is denied by default, unless the IPFIREWALL_DEFAULT_TO_ACCEPT option is set in the kernel configuration. This option should not be set on the gateway.

Place the completed script in */etc/firewall.conf*, mark it as executable using *chmod*, and call it from the *rc.local* file. It will then be called when the system starts up.

If you find after a while that all the spurious traffic with spoofed source IP addresses is filling up your logs, consider removing the log command from some of the rules in this ruleset.

Unfortunately, at the time of this writing there does not appear to be a feasible way to perform MAC address filtering on FreeBSD. Pekka Nikander at Ericsson has begun to develop this capability along with 802.1x support. A paper describing this work can be found at *http://www.tml.hut.fi/~pnr/publications/Freenix2002-Nikander.pdf*

Rate Limiting

FreeBSD has an easy-to-use ability to limit the rate of a subset of traffic. This is provided by the Dummynet system. The most likely use for this in a wireless deployment is to limit how much traffic users of the wireless network can pass to the Internet. There are two steps to enabling Dummynet. First, kernel support for it has to be enabled with the following option in the kernel configuration:

```
options DUMMYNET
```

After compiling the kernel with that option, two new rules have to be added at the start of our firewall script. These two rules should be placed after the variable definitions, but before all of the other add rules:

```
${fwcmd} add pipe 1 ip from ${wif} to any via ${oif}
${fwcmd} pipe 1 config bw 100Kbit/s
```

The first rule creates a new pipe that will channel all traffic from the wireless interface to the outside interface. The second rule configures that pipe with a bandwidth (bw) limitation of 100 KBit/s. This number can be adjusted to reflect how much bandwidth the wireless network should have access to.

The first rule, the one that creates the pipes, will show up with all the other rules when the *ipfw list* command is given. To see the actual configuration of pipes however, *ipfw pipe list* needs to be used.

DHCP

The DHCP daemon will provide automatic assignment of IP addresses to hosts on the local wired and wireless networks. Make sure that the *dhcpd* service has been enabled. If it is not installed on your system, you can get the latest version from *http://www.isc.org/products/DHCP/*, or install it using the ports system by making */usr/ports/net/isc-dhcp3*.

The configuration of the DHCP daemon is stored in the file */etc/dhcpd.conf*. Edit this file to contain:

```
subnet 192.0.2.0 netmask 255.255.255.0 {
        not authoritative;
}

subnet 192.168.0.0 netmask 255.255.255.0 {
```

```
        option domain-name-servers 192.0.2.3;
        option routers 192.168.0.1;
        range 192.168.0.100 192.168.0.200;
}

subnet 192.168.1.0 netmask 255.255.255.0 {
        option domain-name-servers 192.0.2.3;
        option routers 192.168.1.1;
        range 192.168.1.100 192.168.1.200;
}
```

The three subnet clauses in this file correspond to the three interfaces on the gateway.

Ensure that the subnet address and net mask of the first clause match that of the interface connected to your upstream provider. The statement not authoritative tells the DHCP daemon not to assign DHCP addresses on that interface.

The other two clauses will be used to assign addresses to the clients on the 192.168. 0.0 and 192.168.1.0 networks. The option routers statement will tell the clients to use the IP address of the corresponding gateway interface as a router for outbound traffic. The option domain-name-servers statement tells the clients what DNS server to use. Change this to be the DNS server provided by your ISP. If you want to run a caching DNS server as described in the next section, change it to match the address in the option routers statement.

DNS

In the DHCP configuration outlined in the previous section, the clients are sent the upstream provider's DNS server IP addresses. This is the simplest way to set things up, but you might want to go to a step further and run your own DNS server.

There are two common reasons to run your own DNS server: caching DNS lookups for performance reasons or hosting a domain. DNS caching can improve performance by handling repeated DNS lookups locally. This probably won't make a very big difference unless your upstream DNS server has noticeable delays. The proper hosting of a domain is a more advanced topic; if you wish to do this, you should consult the DNS server documentation for information on configuration.

By running DNS as an additional service on the gateway, a new potential point of vulnerability is introduced. BIND, the most widely used DNS server, has a history of security issues. To help limit exposure, it should be set up in a *chroot* environment. The latest version of BIND and documentation can be found at *http://www.isc.org/ products/BIND/*.

FreeBSD has a caching DNS server that can be enabled fairly easily. Set the following:

```
named_enable="YES"
```

in *letc/rc.conf*, and it will start at boot time. Note that this is not *chrooted* by default. The man pages will provide information on how to set this up to be *chrooted*.

If you do decide to configure the gateway with a caching DNS server, make sure you change the DHCP configuration file to give the proper gateway IP addresses in option domain-name-server. The address will be different for the wired and wireless segments as the gateway's two interfaces for those segments have different IP addresses. The DNS server should also have zone files to handle reverse lookups on your internal address space by the clients.

Static ARP

ARP poisoning attacks, discussed in Chapter 2, are a real threat to all entities on a wireless network, including the gateway. An ARP attack against the gateway could cut off all network connectivity to the clients. The possibility of a successful ARP attack can be reduced by setting up static ARP entries for IP addresses that we know ahead of time.

In the case of the gateway, two particular IP addresses can benefit most from static ARP: the IP of the access point and the IP of the cable modem or router.

Add two lines to the end of *letc/rc.local*:

```
arp -S <AP IP> <AP MAC>
arp -S <ROUTER IP> <ROUTER MAC>
```

If there are any hosts on the wired network that are going to act as servers and will not be using DHCP to get dynamic addresses, it wouldn't hurt to create static ARP entries for them too.

Auditing

Proper auditing is even more important on the gateway than it is on the client machines. The gateway is the contact point with the outside world, and it will receive nonstop abuse from all over the Internet. Because of this, it's vital to keep a good eye on the logs of this machine.

The services *arpwatch*, *syslog*, and *swatch* should all be installed and configured in the same fashion as described for the FreeBSD client machines in Chapter 4.

Don't forget to periodically log in to the gateway and check the logs and root user mail for evidence of a security breach. Or even better, forward this information to an email account you check often.

At this point, everything should be all set on the gateway. It's a good idea to reboot and make sure all the services start up without any errors. Fire up a wireless client, and check to make sure it gets an IP address and can access the Internet.

CHAPTER 13

Building an OpenBSD Gateway

Given the similarities between OpenBSD and FreeBSD, one would assume that the gateway configuration would be nearly identical for each of them. However, due to the underlying differences in kernel configuration and firewall structure, the implementation is surprisingly different in FreeBSD. The end result, however, is the same; a secured and efficient gateway machine protecting your wireless network.

Like FreeBSD, we will use dc0, dc1, and dc2 as the network interfaces. These correspond to the common *Netgear* and *Linksys* cards sold in most stores. Replace these with the names you have created for the three interfaces.

Building the Gateway

Your layer 3 gateway is your primary line of defense from outside attackers. It can also be a valuable threat in keeping wireless attackers at bay. The gateway effectively controls the keys to your networked kingdom. Due to the central role the gateway plays in your network, special care should be taken throughout the installation and configuration process. A hole left in your gateway is a hole into your network.

When installing OpenBSD, make sure you install the kernel source code. Also, unless absolutely necessary, do not install the X Windows system. There are many SUID binaries installed at part of X and several programs bind to externally reachable ports on your machine. Not installing X Windows greatly simplifies the maintenance of your machine. Also, be sure to have a sufficiently large */var* file system to accommodate your logging requirements. 500 megabytes should be reasonable for a DSL-connected host.

Once the operating system is installed, examine the OpenBSD web site for security issues with your release. Links to various security vulnerabilities can be found at *http://www.openbsd.org/security.html*. Follow the instructions in the advisories to apply any required patches. If there are numerous vulnerabilities to be patched on your system, you may want to update your system to the –stable branch, otherwise known as the "patch branch." The –stable branch of your release is a part of the OpenBSD release cycle which keeps the latest security and reliability patches in an already released version of the operating system. For more information on the –stable branch and upgrading to it, see http://www.openbsd.org/stable.html.

OpenBSD Kernel Configuration

The kernel must be configured for use as a gateway. The kernel should be stripped of any unneeded options or devices. This not only adds to the security of the kernel but also keeps the kernel small and fast. For complete details on compiling a secure OpenBSD kernel, see Chapter 6.

Once the kernel has been locked down, gateway-specific options need to be added to the kernel configuration. Firewall support is required to allow for stateful packet filtering. Also, packet-forwarding support must be added to allow the gateway to properly route packets between interfaces. Finally, IPsec support should be added to allow for VPN connections from the wireless network. Add the following lines to the architecture-independent configuration file:

```
option          GATEWAY          # packet forwarding
option          IPSEC            # IPsec
pseudo-device   pf       1       # packet filter
pseudo-device   pflog    1       # pf log if
```

Compile and install your new kernel and verify the host acts properly after a reboot. If the gateway is going to connect to the wireless network using *HostAP* or a wireless network card instead of an Ethernet connection to the AP, make sure the kernel has support for the wireless drivers selected and has the proper options set. The options are described in "Wireless Kernel Configuration" in Chapter 6 and the *HostAP* instructions of Chapter 9.

Configuring Services

Just as with a wireless client, unneeded services should be disabled to reduce the risk of running vulnerable services. For a complete discussion of removing services under OpenBSD, see "Disable Unneeded Services" in Chapter 6.

Once unneeded services have been disabled, the remaining services and interfaces need to be configured. First, all the interfaces must be configured and a default route added. OpenBSD uses *hostname.<interface>* files to store information about the configuration of each interface. This *hostname.dc0* file represents our external interface. During boot time, this file will give the interface an IP address and set our default route:

```
# Example hostname.dc0
inet 192.0.2.240 255.255.255.0 192.0.2.255
!route add default 192.0.2.1
```

Simple *hostname.dc1* and *hostname.dc2* files configure the other interfaces:

```
# Example hostname.dc1
inet 192.168.0.1 255.255.255.0 192.168.0.255

# Example hostname.dc2
inet 192.168.1.1 255.255.255.0 192.168.1.255
```

It is helpful to place external labels on the interfaces to keep track of which cable goes in where. With three interfaces on a host, it is easy to get confused as to which interface is the external and which is the trusted internal. Putting a label on the card now will save trouble down the road.

By default, an OpenBSD installation does not allow packets to be forwarded between interfaces. Packet forwarding must be turned on at boot time by adding the following line to */etc/sysctl.conf*:

```
net.inet.ip.forwarding=1       # 1=Permit forwarding (routing) of packets
```

If you do not want to wait for a reboot, you can turn on IP forwarding by hand with the following command:

```
# sysctl -w net.inet.ip.forwarding=1
```

Like FreeBSD, OpenBSD has different kernel security levels. The security levels range from -1 (least secure) to 2 (most secure). Ideally, you should run your gateway at secure level 2 once it is in production. When at secure level 2, the packet filter rules cannot be changed at runtime, and the clock cannot be set backwards. Secure level 2 may be a difficult level to run at while configuring a host, so running at level 1 until the host is deployed is advisable. To set the secure level to 2, add the following line to */etc/sysctl.conf*:

```
kern.securelevel=2
```

Finally, the packet filter must be enabled in */etc/rc.conf* by adding the following line:

```
pf=YES              # Packet filter / NAT
```

Reboot the host one final time to make sure the host is responsive and capable of being configured.

Building the Firewall Rules

With the host locked down, the firewall rules must be configured and tested. In our example, there is an external interface, a DMZ interface, and an interface that faces the wireless network. The following firewall rules are very aggressive at limiting communication. The gateway must protect the DMZ from attacks coming from both the Internet and the wireless network. It must also protect the wireless network from attacks originating on the Internet. These requirements lead to a restrictive ruleset that errs on the side of caution.

The firewall rules on an OpenBSD host are normally stored in *letc/pf.conf*. We will examine our firewall script in sections to help explain the thought process that led to this ruleset.

These four variables correspond to your outside interface, network, number of bits in the netmask, and IP address, respectively. Change these to the correct values.

```
# set these to your outside interface network and netmask and ip
o_if = "dc0"
o_net = "192.0.2.0"
o_mask = "24"
o_ip = "192.0.2.230"
```

These variables do the same thing for the wireless network (variables starting with "w") and for the internal wired network (variables starting with "i"). Change these if you are going to use different IP ranges on these networks.

```
# set these to your inside interface networks, netmasks, and IPs
w_if = "dc1"
w_net = "192.168.0.0"
w_mask = "24"
w_ip = "192.168.0.1"

i_if = "dc2"
i_net = "192.168.1.0"
i_mask = "24"
i_ip = "192.168.1.1"
```

The parsing of OpenBSD's *pf* rules differs dramatically from the *ipfw* rules used in FreeBSD. In FreeBSD, the first rule that is matched by the firewall is used to process the packet. In OpenBSD, it is the last rule matched that matters. You can force the packet to exit the ruleset by using the keyword quick. When a packet is matched by a quick rule, the parsing stops and the packet is acted upon by the matched rule.

To have a deny-all ruleset, place the default-blocking rule at the top of the ruleset.

```
# Default deny
block in log all
block out log all
```

These rules allow traffic to and from the loopback interface to pass through the firewall. This allows any connections that are made to *localhost* by internal processes to be successful.

```
# Let loopback traffic through
pass out quick on lo0 all
pass in quick on lo0 all
```

These rules prevent spoofed packets from being passed through the firewall. A spoofed packet is a packet that appears to be from one of our three networks but actually originates on the wrong network. For example, a packet with the source IP of a wireless client should not come into the gateway from the wired network or the external network.

```
# Stop Spoofing
block in quick on $o_if inet from { $i_net/$i_mask, $w_net/$w_mask } to any
block in quick on $i_if inet from { $o_net/$o_mask, $w_net/$w_mask } to any
block in quick on $w_if inet from { $i_net/$i_mask, $o_net/$o_mask } to any
```

This rule blocks incoming packets from the Internet destined to improper network IP ranges such as non-routable, multicast, and broadcast IP addresses.

```
# Stop RFC 1918 et al.
block in quick on $o_if inet from { 127.0.0.0/8, 192.168.0.0/16, \
   10.0.0.0/8, 172.16.0.0/12, 0.0.0.0/8, 169.254.0.0/16, 224.0.0.0/4, \
   240.0.0.0/4 } to any
```

The rule allows clients on the DMZ and wireless networks to query the caching nameserver running on the gateway. The caching nameserver is configured in the "DNS" section later in this chapter.

```
# allow DNS queries to our gateway
pass in quick proto udp from any to { $i_ip, $o_ip, $w_ip } port 53 keep state
```

Allow connections to the SSH daemon from anywhere. This will allow secure administration of the gateway from anyplace the operator may be.

```
# Allow SSH connection
pass in quick proto tcp from any to { $i_ip, $o_ip, $w_ip } port 22 flags S/SA \
   keep state
```

This rule will log and block all attempted TCP setup attempts against the external interface.

```
# Reject and log all setup of incoming connections from the outside
block in log quick proto tcp on $o_if from any to any flags S/SA
```

These rules prevent communication between the wireless network and the DMZ. The wireless network may contain attackers attempting to subvert your firewall in an effort to get to the DMZ. The DMZ must protect itself from the wireless network as if it were the Internet.

```
# Reject connections between the wireless network and DMZ network
block in quick on $w_if inet from any to $i_net/$i_mask
block in quick on $i_if inet from any to $w_net/$w_mask
```

These rules allow outbound connections from the DMZ and wireless networks to the rest of the network. We are allowing the outbound connections that are sourced from the external IP address of the gateway with the assumption that the NAT rules will be configured to use that IP address. Note that since the connections are outbound on the outside interface, the connections to the gateway itself are still dropped. Also, any other connections not explicitly allowed in this ruleset are now dropped by the block-all rule at the top.

```
# Allow all outbound connections from the DMZ and wireless networks
pass in quick on $w_if proto tcp from $w_net/$w_mask to any flags S/SA keep state
pass in quick on $w_if proto { udp, icmp } from $w_net/$w_mask to any keep state
pass in quick on $i_if proto tcp from $i_net/$i_mask to any flags S/SA keep state
pass in quick on $i_if proto { udp, icmp } from $i_net/$i_mask to any keep state
```

```
pass out quick on $o_if proto tcp from $o_ip to any flags S/SA keep state
pass out quick on $o_if proto { udp, icmp } from $o_ip to any keep state
```

Rules stored in *letc/pf.conf* will be loaded at boot time. If you make a change to the firewall rules and want to update them at runtime, use the *pfctl* utility. These commands will flush the firewall rules and then reload them:

```
# pfctl -F rules
# pfctl -R /etc/pf.conf
```

Configuring NAT

The reality of deploying a network in this day and age is that you will end up needing to translate your internal networks to a limited number of public IP addresses. The process, called Network Address Translation (NAT) can be a very complicated process on some operating systems. Thankfully, on OpenBSD it is straightforward procedure with a very robust feature set. Rather than run NAT as a userland process, NAT support is provided directly by the kernel through the packet filter that also provides firewalling capabilities.

The NAT configuration is controlled by directives stored in *letc/nat.con*f. Here is the example file that corresponds with the previous firewall ruleset:

```
# /etc/natd.conf
nat on dc0 from 192.168.0.0/24 to any -> dc0
nat on dc0 from 192.168.1.0/24 to any -> dc0
```

This configuration causes NAT to act on packets that cross the dc0 interface. Any packet from either internal network will be translated to the IP address of the outside interface. This is a very simple configuration. OpenBSD can perform bidirectional NAT'ing where one internal IP address maps to one external IP address. There is also a redirection capability within the NAT implementation to allow for source and destination port manipulation. For a complete listing and explanation of NAT, see the *nat.conf* manual page.

If you make a change to *nat.conf*, you can force the packet filter to reload the rules using the *pfctl* utility. The following command will flush the old NAT rules and load the new ones from *letc/nat.conf*:

```
# pfctl -F nat
# pfctl -N /etc/nat.conf
```

Rate Limiting

OpenBSD provides a robust mechanism for providing rate limiting and Quality of Service (QoS) when the host is acting as a gateway. When supplying bandwidth to a wireless and DMZ network through the same gateway, you generally want the DMZ to have higher priority access to the Internet. This will prevent wireless users from saturating your bandwidth and denying access to your DMZ resources from the outside.

The OpenBSD queuing interface, ALTQ, allows for many different types of traffic shaping. Class Based Queuing (CBQ) and Random Early Detection (RED) are enabled by default in a standard OpenBSD installation. To make sure they are enabled, check your platform independent kernel configuration file for the following line:

```
option ALTQ
```

ALTQ is controlled by a userland daemon called *altqd*. *altqd* reads its configuration from */etc/altq.conf* by default. To ensure *altqd* starts at boot time, verify the following line is contained in your */etc/rc.conf*:

```
altqd_flags=""
```

More advanced QoS mechanisms such as Hierarchical Fair Service Curve (HFSC), Weighted Fair Queuing (WFQ) and Priority Queuing (PRIQ) can be turned on using various configuration options. For a full list of the queuing options, see the *options(4)* manual page.

With CBQ, you can create classes of traffic based on source or destination protocols and addresses. These classes can be very generic and cover whole subnets or they can be very specific and apply only to a certain TCP port on a given server. These classes can then be assigned a percentage or absolute amount of the total available bandwidth.

One of the largest offenders of excessive bandwidth utilization on a corporate network is web surfing. We will use web-surfing limitation as our example. First, the maximum available throughput and queuing type must be configured on the external interface. Assume this system has a T1 for connectivity to the Internet:

```
# Example altq.conf
interface dc0 bandwidth 1540K cbq
```

Now the root class must be configured. All other classes will be members of other classes and ultimately a member of the root class. This tree of classes allows for fine-grained control of traffic on various ports in various networks:

```
class cbq dc0 root_class NULL priority 0 pbandwidth 100
```

The *root_class* parent is set to NULL since there are no other classes. The priority is set to 0, the lowest. pbandwidth is the percentage of the available bandwidth the class can use. In this case, the *root_class* is allowed all the available bandwidth.

Now a default child class must be created to serve as a catchall for other, non-classified traffic:

```
class cbq dc0 def_class root_class borrow pbandwidth 100 default
```

The *def_class* is a child of the *root_class*. The keyword borrow indicates this class can borrow spare bandwidth from its parent class. If the borrow keyword is omitted, the percentage bandwidth would be an maximum bandwidth, not simply a guaranteed bandwidth. The default keyword indicates this is the catchall class.

Finally, a web-surfing class must be created:

```
class cbq dc0 ws_class def_class pbandwidth 20 red
```

ws_class is a child of *def_class* and will only be allowed to use a maximum of 20% of the available bandwidth. If the 20% cap is violated, the kernel will use RED to throttle down connections.

For the *ws_class*, filter definitions must be created to instruct the kernel how to apply this class. Filters take the following structure:

```
filter dst_address [netmask netmask] dst_port src_address [netmask netmask] \
    src_port protocol
```

The protocol is the IP protocol number (e.g., TCP is IP protocol number 6). The value 0 serves as a wildcard for *altq* filters. The following rules will limit web surfing, which originates from our NAT address:

```
filter dc0 wi_class 192.0.2.230 0 0 80 0
filter dc0 wi_class 0 80 192.0.2.230 0 0
```

altqd may be started by hand. Check your *syslog* files for any configuration error which *altqd* will log as start time. By examining your firewall logs and utilization statistics, you will be able to determine what traffic is important to your network and what traffic is causing unneeded performance problems. Using ALTQ, you can classify and shape the traffic coming in and out of your network to get the most out of your resources.

DHCP

DHCP will be used to assign IP addresses, nameserver information, and routes to clients on both the wired and wireless networks. The DHCP server daemon comes installed but turned off in a default OpenBSD installation. In order to turn on *dhcpd*, modify the *dhcpd* line in */etc/rc.conf* to be the following:

```
dhcpd_flags="-q"
```

The q flag keeps *dhcpd* from printing various copyright information at boot time. For a complete discussion on the configuration of DHCP on a gateway server, see "DHCP" in Chapter 11.

DNS

Like FreeBSD, OpenBSD has a nameserver installed by default. This allows for easy configuration of a caching nameserver. A caching nameserver is not authoritative for any domain; it simply serves as a recursive resolver for clients.

OpenBSD runs an older yet heavily audited version of BIND, the popular nameserver from ISC. While many other operating systems are shipping with BIND 9.x, OpenBSD 3.1 runs BIND 4.9.8. Version 4 BIND installations use legacy configuration files and maintenance mechanisms. For more information on BIND, see *http://www.isc.org/products/BIND/*. By default, the nameserver on OpenBSD runs in a *chroot'd* jail.

chroot is a mechanism for changing what a process considers to be the root of the file system. A *chroot'd* process will, for instance, think that */var/named* is really /. *chroot'ing* a process greatly reduces the risk to the host in the event of a compromise. A properly *chroot'd* jail will keep attackers limited to the jail. They will not be able to break out to affect the rest of the system.

To turn on OpenBSD's caching nameserver, modify the *named_flags* option to be the following:

```
named_flags=""
```

After the next reboot, the system will be running a caching nameserver. From a client on the network you should be able to use a utility such as *nslookup* to verify the process is acting as expected.

Static ARP

ARP poisoning attacks, such as those described in Chapter 2, are a real threat to all entities in the same broadcast domain including the gateway. By adding static ARP entries on your gateway for sensitive hosts, you reduce the risk posed by an ARP poisoning attack. In particular, static entries should be made for the default gateway, for any access points, and any servers that exist on your wired network. These entries will protect the gateway from participating in an ARP attack against your primary infrastructure. For instructions on creating static ARP entries at boot time, see "Static ARP Entries" in Chapter 6.

Auditing

Even after configuring your gateway in a secure a manner as possible, there is still a chance of compromise of the machine. Without proper audit trail creation and regular examination of the audit trail, you may never know if the host has been compromised or misconfigured over time.

The services *arpwatch*, *syslog*, and *swatch* should all be installed and configured in the same fashion as described for the FreeBSD client machines in Chapter 4.

Don't forget to periodically log in to the gateway and check the logs and root user mail for evidence of a security breach. Or even better, forward this information to an email account you check often.

Now that your gateway is fully configured, be sure to test access from the wired and wireless segments. You may need to fine-tune firewall rules to give you the access you need. OpenBSD is a secure and robust operating system. An OpenBSD gateway is can be an excellent first line of defense if configured and maintained properly.

## CHAPTER 14

Authentication and Encryption

WEP provides a basic layer of encryption for traffic in 802.11 networks. But, even beyond the previously discussed problems of WEP, it does not provide authentication or integrity checks of the data on the network. There are several other tools that can be used to bolster the security of the network by providing these services. Using them individually, or in conjunction, can add important safeguards.

This chapter will discuss portals, IPsec, and 802.1x. Each of these performs a different function. Portals are designed to require a high-level authentication, such as a username and password, before allowing traffic out of the local network. IPsec can be used to encrypt and authenticate traffic on a per-packet basis. Finally, 802.1x is used to authenticate connected hardware at layer 2, limiting what devices can utilize a network. 802.1x is also being used to distribute WEP keys for some vendors' hardware.

Portals

A captive portal is a router or gateway host that will not allow traffic to pass until authentication conditions are met. They see wide use commercially in pay-for-use public access networks, such as those found in hotels and airports. Their operation of a captive portal breaks down to a few simple steps:

1. Assign a new computer on the network an IP address through DHCP.
2. Block all traffic, except to the captive portal server.
3. Redirect any web traffic the new user attempts to the captive portal.
4. Display terms of use, billing information, and/or a login screen.
5. Once the user has accepted the terms, or logged in, allow them access.
6. Optionally: When some defined amount of time has passed, remove their access.

There are several different ways of using a captive portal. Closed captive portals can be used either for limiting access only to a known set of users with usernames and passwords or for requiring payment before service is established. Another form of captive portal used primarily in the community wireless networking model, the open captive portal, simply requires acceptance of the terms of use before access is granted.

Several commercial products can provide captive portal functionality. Starting in the summer of 2001, open source programmers involved with wireless networking who realized the need for using captive portals sought to create software-based portals that would run on Linux and BSD servers. To give an overview of open source captive portals, we will examine two software packages, *NoCat* and *WiCap*. *NoCat* is a full-featured, and complex to deploy, captive portal that can handle operating in both closed and open modes and supports central authentication servers. *WiCap* is a much simpler captive portal, written as Perl scripts for OpenBSD. It only runs as an open portal and offers time-limited access to anyone.

NoCat

NoCat provides support for both closed (captive or passive in their terminology) and open modes. When running in closed mode *NoCat* uses encrypted communications with a central authentication server to validate passwords. This allows multiple portal servers throughout an infrastructure to tie into to one common authentication system. *NoCat* currently runs on Linux, FreeBSD, and OpenBSD.

To set up *NoCat*, first download the latest version from *http://nocat.net/*. Unpack it, and build the software. The command:

```
make gateway
```

should build and install *NoCat* into */usr/local*. *NoCat* is configured by editing the file */usr/local/nocat/gateway.conf*. The variable *GatewayMode* in this file determines whether the portal will be of type captive, passive, or open. Captive mode will make it behave as closed server requiring authentication. Passive does the same but works behind NAT gateways. Open places the portal in mode that displays a splash screen or terms of use but does not require any authentication or a centralized server.

Configure the rest of the settings following the directions in the documentation. If you run the server in captive or passive mode, be sure to set up an authentication server and configure that properly as well. This is more complex, and you should refer to the documentation for the most up-to-date options for configuring the server.

To start the gateway, run:

```
/usr/local/bin/gateway
```

WiCap

WiCap was developed to provide simple open portal services on OpenBSD. It consists of web pages and a CGI script for Apache that display terms of use and allow a user to accept. After the user accepts, it modifies the *pf* firewall ruleset to allow the new machine access. It uses the OpenBSD NAT facilities to redirect all unauthenticated traffic to the portal web server.

Setup is quite simple. The configuration files are copied to */etc*, the scripts installed in a binary directory, and the web pages and CGI script installed into the Apache document directory. The configuration files should all be edited to suit how you want the portal to function and to tune firewall rules and the displayed web page.

WiCap is still a rudimentary program, but it provides an excellent system to examine to get a better understanding of the basic functioning of a captive portal, primarily because it is much simpler than *NoCat*. It would make a good foundation for a custom set of scripts and will likely improve in functionality with time, as more people use it and contribute their additions. It can be downloaded from *http://www. geekspeed.net/wicap*.

IPsec VPN

IPsec is a very powerful protocol. Properly used, it can provide a high degree of integrity and confidentiality of data transiting a network. Since these are two traits wireless networks generally do not have, IPsec is a natural supplement for wireless networks.

Unfortunately, like any protocol as powerful as IPsec is, it can be difficult to set up. There are many different parts of the IPsec protocol and many configurable options. However, if your network requires the high levels of security IPsec offers, then fighting through the setup is worth the effort. A word of advice: if possible, try to start with a homogeneous IPsec environment. For your first IPsec connection, attempt to connect two machines of the same operating system. While there is only one IPsec protocol, there are many different ways to configure and use it. It is much easier to configure a FreeBSD to FreeBSD IPsec tunnel than a FreeBSD to Linux tunnel.

This section is designed to be a crash course in setting up a VPN on your wireless network. For a more thorough presentation of setting up an IPsec VPN, visit Tina Bird's VPN web site at *http://vpn.shmoo.com/*.

IPsec in a Nutshell

IPsec can operate in two different modes. *Transport* mode is used to send protected traffic between two nodes. A gateway between two endpoints cannot perform transparent mode encryption. In transparent mode, a new header is placed on the original IP packet to allow for the cryptographic functions to be applied to the packet. An IPsec connection can also be made in *tunnel* mode. A tunnel connection encapsulates an entire IP packet within another IP packet. This allows an intermediate gateway to provide IPsec protection to an entire network. Tunnel mode is the appropriate mode for a VPN connection between a station and egress gateway. The rest of the discussion here will focus on tunnel mode connections.

There are two protocols at the core of IPsec. Authenticated Header (AH) provides authentication and integrity verification of an IP packet. It does not provide confidentiality for the data contained within a packet. Encapsulated Security Payload (ESP) provides confidentiality of the data contained. ESP and AH can be used on their own or in conjunction depending on your security requirements. Given the risk posed by using a wireless network, it is recommended that both protocols be used.

A Security Association (SA) is a unidirectional relationship between two IPsec peers. In order for traffic to flow back and forth between two hosts within an IPsec tunnel, an SA must exist for each direction. The SA includes information about what type of connection exists, what cryptographic algorithms are being utilized, and the keys that are used. A Security Policy Database (SPD) is a list of all security policies installed on a machine. A security policy is a description of a unidirectional connection between two peers including networks to be sent over the IPsec connection and whether the connection should be secured with AH or ESP or both.

Setting up an SA by hand can be a difficult and time-consuming task. Setting up multiple SAs for multiple hosts on a network would be down right annoying. Thankfully, the Internet Key Exchange protocol (IKE) can handle the creation of SAs for us. IKE is the result of several protocols and procedures being unified under one protocol. IKE configuration can get extremely complicated when interoperating between two different IPsec implementations. For your wireless network, keep it simple and get everything working first. Once your IPsec connection is up and running, then tune IKE.

 IKE uses UDP port 500. Make sure you are allowing UDP port 500 between hosts that are attempting to setup an IPsec connection.

In a general-purpose wireless network, the wireless medium is the least trustworthy part of the entire flow between two hosts. In order to overcome this, IPsec can be run on all stations in tunnel mode with ESP and AH for both authentication and confidentiality. The termination of the tunnel is the network gateway, usually a firewall. Even if an attacker breaks your WEP key, the IPsec protection should protect at least the payload of your traffic from being decrypted.

FreeBSD IPsec Implementation

Using IPsec with IKE under FreeBSD requires enabling IPsec in the kernel as well as installing a userland program, *racoon*, to handle the IKE negotiations.

Compile a custom kernel with IPsec support:

```
options        IPSEC            #IP security
options        IPSEC_ESP        #IP security (crypto; define w/ IPSEC)
options        IPSEC_DEBUG      #debug for IP security
```

Build and install the kernel. Reboot to verify it works.

racoon can be installed using the network section of the ports tree or can be downloaded from *ftp://ftp.kame.net/pub/kame/misc/*. Install *racoon* per the instructions provided with the distribution at *http://www.kame.net/*, and in particular *http://www.kame.net/newsletter/20001119/*.

FreeBSD IPsec Client Configuration

On the station, first you should configure *racoon*. You will need to modify this example *racoon.conf* to suit your needs:

```
path include "/usr/local/etc/racoon" ;
path pre_shared_key "/usr/local/etc/racoon/psk.txt" ;
remote anonymous
{
        exchange_mode aggressive,main;
        my_identifier user_fqdn "user1@domain.com";
        lifetime time 1 hour;
        initial_contact on;

        proposal {
                encryption_algorithm 3des;
                hash_algorithm sha1;
                authentication_method pre_shared_key ;
                dh_group 2 ;
        }
}
sainfo anonymous
{
        pfs_group 1;
        lifetime time 30 min;
        encryption_algorithm 3des ;
        authentication_algorithm hmac_sha1;
        compression_algorithm deflate ;
}
```

In your firewall configuration, be sure you allow IKE connections to your machine. *racoon* needs to be configured to start at boot time. Save the following script in */usr/local/etc/rc.d/racoon.sh*:

```
#!/bin/sh
# This script will start racoon in FreeBSD
case "$1" in
start)
# start racoon
    echo -n 'starting racoon'
```

```
    /usr/local/sbin/racoon
    ;;

stop)
# Delete the MAC address from the ARP table
    echo 'stopping racoon'
    killall racoon
    ;;
*)
# Standard usage statement
    echo "Usage: `basename $0` {start|stop}" >&2
    ;;
esac

exit 0
```

Make sure the file is executable by performing

```
chmod 755 /usr/local/etc/rc.d/racoon.sh
```

The */usr/local/etc/racoon/psk.txt* file contains your credentials. This file must be read-able only by root. If the permissions are not set correctly, racoon will not function. For a shared-secret IPsec connection, the file contains your identification (in this case your email address) and the secret. For instance, you can setup a *psk.txt* as the following:

```
user1@domain.com       supersecret
```

Finally, you must set up the security policy. This is done using the *setkey* utility to add entries to the kernel SPD. Create the following *client.spd* that can be loaded by *setkey*. For this setup, the station IP is 192.168.0.104 and the gateway is 192.168.0.1:

```
spdadd 192.168.0.104/32 0.0.0.0/0 any -P out ipsec esp/tunnel/192.168.0.104-192.168.
0.1/require ;
spdadd 0.0.0.0/0 192.168.0.104/32 any -P in ipsec esp/tunnel/192.168.0.1-192.168
.0.104/require ;
```

The first entry creates a security policy that sends all traffic to the VPN endpoint. The second entry creates a security policy that allows all traffic back from the VPN endpoint. Note that in this configuration the client is unable to talk to any hosts on the local subnet besides the VPN gateway. In a wireless network where the client is a prime target for attack, this is a probably a good thing for your workstation.

Load the SPD by running:

```
setkey -f client.spd
```

FreeBSD IPsec Gateway Configuration

For the gateway, *racoon.conf* is the same as the client side. This allows any client to connect. The *psk.txt* file must contain all the identification and shared secrets of all clients who may connect. For instance:

```
user1@domain.com       supersecret
```

```
user2@domain.com        evenmoresecret
user3@domain.com        notsosecret
```

Again, make sure *psk.txt* is readable only by root. Start *racoon* and make sure there are no errors. Finally, create a *gateway.spd* that creates SPD for each client. Assume your clients are at `192.168.0.10[4-6]`:

```
spdadd 0.0.0.0/0 192.168.0.104/32 any -P out ipsec esp/tunnel/192.168.0.1-192.168
.0.104/require ;
spdadd 192.168.0.104/32 0.0.0.0/0 any -P in ipsec esp/tunnel/192.168.0.104-192.168.0.
1/require ;
spdadd 0.0.0.0/0 192.168.0.105/32 any -P in ipsec esp/tunnel/192.168.0.1-192.168
.0.105/require ;
spdadd 192.168.0.105/32 0.0.0.0/0 any -P out ipsec esp/tunnel/192.168.0.105-192.168.
0.1/require ;
spdadd 0.0.0.0/0 192.168.0.106/32 any -P in ipsec esp/tunnel/192.168.0.1-192.168
.0.106/require ;
spdadd 192.168.0.106/32 0.0.0.0/0 any -P out ipsec esp/tunnel/192.168.0.106-192.168.
0.1/require ;
```

Load the SPD by issuing *setkey –f gateway.spd*. Verify the SPD entries using the *spddump* command in *setkey*. At this point, you should be able to ping a wireless client from the gateway. It may take a packet or two for the VPN negotiation to complete, but the connection should be solid after that. If you are unable to ping, examine your *syslog* output for errors and warnings.

 The SPD entries are stored in the kernel. If you have to restart *racoon* due to a configuration change, the SPD entries will still be loaded. The SPD entries are completely controlled via the *setkey* command.

Linux IPsec Implementation

The most popular way of configuring IPsec connections under Linux is using the FreeS/WAN package. FreeS/WAN is made up of two components similar to the FreeBSD implementation. KerneL IP Security (KLIPS) is the kernel level code that actually encrypts and decrypts the data as well as managing the SPD. *pluto* is a userland daemon that controls IKE negotiation. Unlike FreeBSD, both the kernel-level code and userland tools come from outside the core kernel distribution.

The FreeS/WAN build process will build a new kernel and the required management utilities. Download the latest FreeS/WAN source from *http://www.freeswan. org/* and untar the source tree in */usr/src*. The documentation that comes with FreeS/WAN is very extensive and can help you tailor the installation to suit your needs. The kernel component can be installed as either a kernel loadable module or statically compiled directly into your kernel. In order to compile FreeS/WAN, you must have your kernel source installed on your machine. During the compilation process, the kernel configuration utility will launch. This is normal. Compile FreeS/WAN using your kernel configuration method of choice (such the menu-based or X11-

based options). Once the compilation is complete, install the kernel and userland tools per the FreeS/WAN documentation (typically a *make install* will suffice).

FreeS/WAN configuration is controlled by two configuration files: */etc/ipsec.conf* and */etc/ipsec.secrets*. The examples given in this section are very limited in scope to a wireless network. The man pages for both files are quite informative and useful for more complicated connection requirements. An excellent resource for more information is the book *Building Linux Virtual Private Networks*, by Oleg Kolesnikov and Brian Hatch.

Linux IPsec Client Configuration

The *ipsec.conf* file breaks a VPN connection into a right- and left-hand segment. This difference is merely a logical division. The left hand side can be either the internal or external network. This allows the same configuration file to be used for both ends of a VPN network-to-network tunnel. Unfortunately in our case, there will be differences between the client and gateway configurations.

The file is broken up into a configuration section (config) and a connection section (conn). The config section specifies basic parameters for IPsec such as available interfaces as well as specific directives to be passed to *pluto*. The conn section describes the various connections that are available to the VPN. There is a global conn section (conn %default) where you can specify values that are common to all connections such as the lifetime of a key and the method of key exchange.

The following *ipsec.conf* encrypts all information to the Internet with a VPN endpoint on your gateway:

```
# /etc/ipsec.conf
# Set configuration options
config setup
    interfaces=%defaultroute
    # Debug parameters.  Set either to "all" for more info
    klipsdebug=none
    plutodebug=none
    # standard Pluto configuration
    plutoload=%search
    plutostart=%search
    # make sure there are no PMTU Discovery problems
    overridemtu=1443
# default configuration settings
conn %default
    # Be aggressive in rekeying attempts
    keyingtries=0
    # use IKE
    keyexchange=ike
    keylife=12h
    # use shared secrets
    authby=secret
# setup the VPN to the Internet
```

```
conn wireless_connection1
    type=tunnel
    # left is the client side
    left=192.168.0.104
    # right is the internet gateway
    right=192.168.0.1
    rightsubnet=0.0.0.0/0
    # automatically start the connection
    auto=start
```

Now add the shared secret to *ipsec.secrets*:

```
192.168.0.104 192.168.0.1: PSK "supersecret"
```

That is it. Once your gateway is configured, try to ping your default gateway. *pluto* will launch automatically and the connection should come up. If you have a problem reaching the gateway, check the *syslog* messages on both the client and gateway.

Linux IPsec Gateway Configuration

The gateway configuration is largely the same as the client configuration. Given the intelligence of the *ipsec.conf* file, there are very few changes that need to be made. Since your gateway has more than one ethernet interface, you should hard-set the IPsec configuration to use the right interface:

```
# assume internal ethernet interface is eth0
interfaces="ipsec0=eth0"
```

You will then need to add a connection for each internal client. This can be handled in different ways as your network scales, but this configuration should work for a reasonable number of clients:

```
...
conn wireless_connection2
    type=tunnel
    left=192.168.0.105
    right=192.168.0.1
    rightsubnet=0.0.0.0/0
    auto=start
conn wireless_connection3
    type=tunnel
    left=192.168.0.106
    right=192.168.0.1
    rightsubnet=0.0.0.0/0
    auto=start
...
```

Finally, add the shared secrets for all the clients to *ipsec.secrets*:

```
192.168.0.105 192.168.0.1: PSK "evenmoresecret"
192.168.0.106 192.168.0.1: PSK "notsosecret"
```

Clients should now be connecting to the Internet via a VPN tunnel to the gateway. Check the log files or turn up the debug level if the tunnel does not come up.

802.1x

The security structure in 802.11, including WEP and WEP-based authentication, is not designed to scale to handle large, public networks. The shared key design in WEP requires the network administrator to trust many users with the same authentication credentials for the same set of access points. A standard 802.11 installation also allows anyone within reach to have full access to the layer 2 environments on either side of the access point, regardless of the presence of a portal at the network gateway.

802.1x, a ratified IEEE standard, solves some but not all of these problems. 802.1x is a port based, extensible authentication protocol. "Port based," in this sense, means a physical port. 802.1x was designed to solve security problems on a campus network. On a typical university campus, there are thousands of Ethernet jacks waiting for someone to plug in and use them. 802.1x was designed to prevent an attacker from walking up to a jack, plugging in, and begin using the network. The protocol is designed to limit the use of the port until the client machine is authenticated.

Structure of 802.1x

There are three players in the 802.1x protocol. The *supplicant* is the client machine attempting to gain access to the network. The *authenticator* is the layer 2 device that is providing the port (such as an Ethernet switch or an 802.11b access point). The *authentication server* is the device that actually verifies the authentication data provided by the supplicant. The relationship of these players is illustrated in Figure 14-1.

The actual authentication protocol used by entities in an 802.1x transaction is called the Extensible Authentication Protocol (EAP). EAP was originally designed as an authentication mechanism for PPP-based connections. However, when the designers of 802.1x were looking for an authentication mechanism, they discovered EAP generally fit their criteria and used it as part of the standard.

EAP is effectively a challenge-response authentication protocol that can be extended to run over any transport mechanism and use any crypto system to handle verification. In the case of wireless networks, the transport is provided by the EAP over LAN protocol (EAPOL). As far as the authentication service, there are many options that can be used, including Remote Authentication Dial In User Service (RADIUS) via Lightweight EAP (LEAP) or Transport Layer Security (TLS) via EAP-TLS. By allowing for different authentication mechanisms, EAP is a future-proof protocol. If, for instance, a weakness is discovered in TLS, then a new authentication mechanism can be fit into EAP without having to abandon the entire protocol. In particular, as long as the authenticator is 802.1x compliant, it should never have to be upgraded when the underlying cryptography changes.

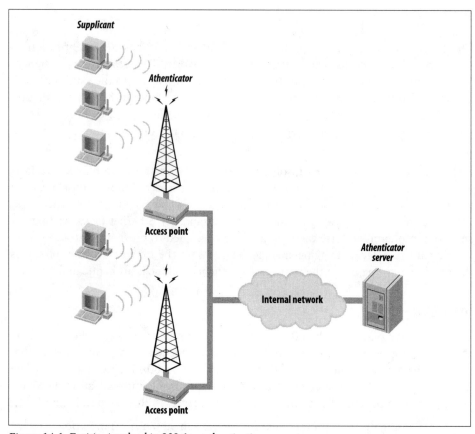

Figure 14-1. Entities involved in 802.1x authentication

When an unauthenticated supplicant connects to an 802.1x-controlled port, the authenticator has the port in a restricted traffic mode. The only traffic allowed across the port is traffic to and from the authentication server. The device is not even allowed to talk to other devices on the same layer 2 network. The supplicant starts the authentication process by sending an EAP-Start message. The authenticator (which, since we are talking about wireless networks, will henceforth be called an access point) sends an EAP request to the supplicant. The supplicant replies with the requested authentication credentials. The access point then forwards the credentials on to the authentication server.

The authentication server attempts to verify the credentials of the supplicant. The authentication may request more information from the supplicant, in which case the EAP-request/response cycle happens again. Once the authentication server is satisfied with the supplicant's credentials, it will send an *accept* or *reject* message to the access point. The access point will then either allow traffic from the supplicant or reject the supplicant based on the answer from the authentication server. This process is shown in Figure 14-2.

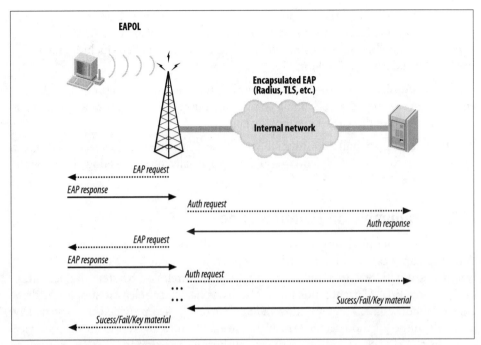

Figure 14-2. 802.1x authentication process

What makes 802.1x so powerful in a wireless network is the fact that data can be shipped from the authentication server to the supplicant along with the accept message. For wireless networks, WEP keys can be sent to the supplicant upon successful authentication. 802.1x also allows for periodic reauthentication of the client machine. Every time the supplicant is forced to reverify itself, the authentication server can send it new WEP keys. This allows for a rapid rotation of WEP keys. Therefore, even if an attacker is attempting to crack the currently used WEP key, there is a very limited amount of traffic that is encrypted using that key.

Limitations of 802.1x

Through the entire discussion of 802.1x you just read through, there was no mention of a new data integrity protocol. 802.1x is strictly an authentication protocol: nothing more, nothing less. It allows wireless users to work around weaknesses in WEP by providing a scalable mechanism to rotate quickly through WEP keys. However, it does not actually fix WEP, it is only a workaround that can reduce the risk of using a WEP-based network.

A paper released by Bill Arbaugh et al. from the University of Maryland (available at *http://www.missl.cs.umd.edu/wireless/1x.pdf*) provides great detail on several security holes present in 802.1x when used in wireless networks. Neither 802.1x nor EAP were designed for use in wireless networks. The protocols were not designed to address the particular threat model wireless networks present. Due to this, various vulnerabilities in 802.1x arise when used in a wireless environment. An attacker can perform any number of attacks on an 802.1x-authenticated client including man-in-the-middle and session hijacking.

802.1x was designed to protect the network infrastructure from attack, not the client machines. A rogue access point or malicious user within radio range of a client can undo much of the security offered by 802.1x.

802.1x is not a silver bullet to solve all wireless security threats. However, it is a great way to raise the bar for potential attackers, especially ones targeting the network infrastructure.

802.1x Equipment and Configuration

At the time of writing, support for 802.1x is still not widespread. The first widely deployed supplicants and authentication servers were from Microsoft. Windows XP was released with 802.1x supplicant support in its wireless subsystem. By default, it can perform EAP-TLS authentication. Microsoft has since released supplicant drivers for Windows 2000 and Windows 98SE. Microsoft also provided the first widely available authentication server. The Windows 2000 Internet Authentication Service contains a RADIUS server and certificate authority that supports 802.1x. For information on these drivers and how they can be configured, see Microsoft's web site at *http://www.microsoft.com/*.

Several vendors have firmware-based access points with 802.1x support, including Cisco, Enterasys, and Orinoco Wireless. See *http://www.enterasys.com/*, *http://www.cisco.com/*, and *http://www.orinocowireless.com/* for more information on the 802.1x-capable products from these vendors.

Thankfully, there are also some open source 802.1x implementations starting to arrive. Researchers at the University of Maryland have written an 802.1x supplicant and authenticator for use with several operating systems including Linux. The supplicant and authenticator can be downloaded from *http://www.open1x.org/*.

Authentication server

Even though there are many different methods of possible authentication using EAP, there are very few available implementations. Currently, the best implementation is from the FreeRADIUS project, which has EAP-TLS built into their RADIUS server. In the future, there may be more options. Check out this book's web site for new developments.

The machine running the authentication server does not need to be a very high-powered machine due to the relatively few requests the machine needs to service. For the sake of simplicity, the authentication server could be your firewall. For larger networks, it is recommended that it be a stand-alone machine. Ideally, you will have two hosts for redundancy. Remember, if you are requiring 802.1x of your clients and your authentication server goes down, no one can join the network.

In order to use EAP-TLS with FreeRADIUS, you will need to download and install OpenSSL from *http://www.openssl.org/*. Perform a standard install per the documentation with the distribution. You will need at least Version 0.9.7 for FreeRADIUS to work properly. Be sure to modify your *openssl.conf* to reflect your organization and contact information.

OpenSSL supplies the crypto libraries used by the RADIUS server. It also will serve as a Certificate Authority for your wireless network. You will need to create a self-signed certificate to act as the root certificate for your PKI infrastructure. Then you will need to generate a certificate for the RADIUS server as well as certificates for supplicants. The easiest way to do this is running the script located at *http://www.missl.cs.umd.edu/wireless/eaptls/doc/CA.all*. This script will take care of all your initial certificate generation needs as well as serve as a template for future client certificates.

The downside of running a EAP-TLS based infrastructure is the fact that you have to run your own certificate authority. For an organization of any size, this is not an issue to be undertaken lightly. There are many issues, technical and otherwise, involved in running a CA. These issues are well outside the scope of this book. If you would like more information on OpenSSL and running a CA, we recommend *Network Security with OpenSSL* by John Viega, et al (O'Reilly).

Once you have OpenSSL installed and configured, download and install the FreeRADIUS server from *http://www.freeradius.org/*. Before you compile the RADIUS server, you will need to modify */usr/src/modules/rlm_eap/types/rlm_eap_tls/Makefile* with your OpenSSL location. Be sure TARGET = rlm_eap_tls is specified in the makefile.

Compile and install the RADIUS server per the instructions in the README file. Once the installation is complete, you will need to modify */etc/raddb/radius.conf* to enable EAP-TLS and specify the location of your certificates. Read through the file and edit where necessary. Also, when creating users in the RADIUS server, be sure they have an Auth-Type of EAP. At this point, you should be able to start the RADIUS server and have a fully functional 802.1x authentication server.

RADIUS is a complicated but robust protocol. It is a flexible platform for triple-A services. A complete discussion of the features and implementation of various

RADIUS servers is outside the scope of this book. For an analysis of RADIUS as well as practical examples, we recommend *RADIUS* by Jonathan Hassell (O'Reilly).

Authenticator

At the time of this writing, the Open1x authenticator is still very beta. Download and install the authenticator per the instructions on the Open1x web site. The authenticator must be running on your wireless access point. The access point should be configured per the instructions provided in Chapter 9.

Once the authenticator is installed, it is started with the *auth* command. *auth* takes the following arguments:

p *or* --serverip <IP>
> This is the IP address of the authentication server.

s *or* --serverdevice <device>
> This is the interface that traffic destined for the authentication server will traverse. This is typically the wired interface, such as eth0.

t *or* --suppdevice <device>
> This parameter specified the interface that the authenticator will receive supplicant traffic on. This is typically the wireless interface, such as wlan0.

o *or* --serverport <port>
> This is the port the authentication server is listening on. For RADIUS, this would be 1812.

Be sure to launch the authenticator in the startup location of your choice.

Supplicant

Once you download the supplicant, compile and install it per the instructions included in the README file. Included in the supplicant distribution are startup scripts for various operating systems including FreeBSD and Linux. Make sure they are installed in the correct location to ensure the supplicant starts at boot time.

There are two major configuration activities. First, you must obtain an x.509 certificate for use with your authentication server. This is a requirement since the only EAP method the supplicant understands is EAP-TLS. The certificate must be in ANS1 DER format and the private key must be in PEM format. You must obtain this certificate from a Certificate Authority trusted by your authentication server.

The configuration file for the supplicant is stored in *etc/1x/1x.conf* by default. The file has the following structure:

```
<network id1>:id = <username>
<network id1>:cert = <user certificate file>
<network id1>:key = <user private key file>
<network id1>:root = <trusted root store>
<network id1>:auth = EAP | none
```

The *<network id>* field is your ESSID. This group of parameters can be repeated for multiple ESSIDs so you can roam from one 802.1x-based network to another.

The fields in the configuration file are as follows:

id

> This is the user ID specified in the certificate, which is typically your email address.

cert

> This it the absolute path to your certificate stored in DER format.

key

> This is the absolute path to your private key stored in PEM format.

root

> This is the absolute path to a PEM encoded file containing your trusted root certificates.

auth

> This can be set to either EAP or none. A setting of EAP means that the supplicant will attempt to authenticate to the specified network. A setting of none will cause the supplicant to treat the network as a non-802.1x network and not attempt EAP authentication.

Now that you have your supplicant configured, you can associate to your network and authenticate via 802.1x through your access point to your FreeRADIUS authentication server.

CHAPTER 15
Putting It All Together

Pieces of a Coherent System

Throughout the book, we have examined wireless security one step at a time, moving from clients all the way through to gateways. The security responsibilities of each of these parts translate into the security of the whole. To recap, lets walk through each of the pieces and list what security role they play.

The client machines must protect themselves from other machines on the network. They must also properly communicate with the access point and the gateway to ensure security. If WEP is being used, the client needs to have the correct keys. If IPsec or 802.1x is being used, the client must support the protocol and be configured properly.

Further up the chain is the access point. Many access points have security issues in their firmware, allowing attacks against their SNMP servers or administration consoles. The services provided by these access points should be minimized, and desired security features such as WEP enabled. If the access point is a *HostAP* system, the computer must also be locked down following standard procedures for securing a server.

The gateway provides separation between the wireless network, any local wired networks, and the Internet. It treats the wireless network and the Internet as untrusted sources of traffic, shielding the wired network from them. It also provides services to computers on the wireless network such as NAT, DHCP, and DNS. IPsec tunnels from wireless clients are terminated at the gateway, and it may act as a captive portal or 802.1x authentication server.

Each of these pieces is vital to the security of the network. Remember that if any one of them fails it can lead to compromises of the network. By having the multiple layers of host security, authentication, and encryption, however, many layers of protection are provided. Each of these layers must breached for an attacker to gain further access, and the layers serve to limit compromises. Defense in depth is a solid security practice, and we hope that this book will help you to implement your system with a layered set of defenses.

User Knowledge

In the end, the network needs to be convenient for users as well as secure. The users are the reason the network is there, and if they can't use the network, it isn't serving its purpose.

Security is often seen as a direct trade-off with convenience, but it does not have to be an either/or situation. If a security mechanism is difficult to use, users will seek to bypass it whenever possible. When security is bypassed, it isn't working. So, when implementing security mechanisms, strive to make them both usable and secure. Security mechanisms don't have to impede usability.

As an example, MAC address filtering is mostly transparent to the end user. It does not impose a burden on them, so most users are not going to try to subvert the filtering. The only time it affects them is when they need to get a new network card added to the filter lists. The burden of work (and inconvenience) for MAC filtering lies with the system administrator. Being the person who implemented the security mechanism, the system administrator will hopefully be diligent in maintaining the list of allowed MAC addresses and not try to defeat his own security mechanism.

A bad example, where security makes it inconvenient for users, is the default method of WEP-key management. The user is responsible for entering the right WEP keys into the system and keeping them up to date. A change to the keys, which should happen on a regular basis, requires every user to change settings or have someone do it for them. The shared static keys of WEP also encourage users to talk about them openly, in an effort to help other users. Automatic key distribution mechanisms and authentication systems that distribute keys help shield the user from the morass of key management and prevent problems.

Authentication systems such as captive portals and 802.1x, which are both discussed in Chapter 14, provide authentication methods to help manage identification of users in a wireless network and authorize use of services. When properly integrated, these tools can provide security that is unobtrusive to users, yet quite robust.

The security pitfalls of wireless networking underscore a problem that has not been well addressed so far: the security of client machines is just as important as the security of servers, firewalls, and networks. Even with all of the widespread worms and attacks against broadband users' home computers, most users do not have a good handle on maintaining the security of their systems. It is important to convey the importance of client security to your users and teach them the basics of host security, so that they can do their part to keep the network secure. At the same time, you should strive to ease as much of this burden on the user as possible.

Wireless networks exaggerate this problem, as they in most cases expose the traffic between the clients and the gateway. This can lead to direct access to client machines without having to pass through the gateway's firewall. VPN software, IPsec tunnels, and WEP are good tools for limiting this exposure, but users need to be aware of the risks. Travelers that use their laptops in hotels, airports, and at conferences need to take special care with their systems, as all of these environments often contain hostile traffic and people actively looking for systems to attack.

Explaining the security mechanisms in use to your users, making sure they understand them, and instilling a sense of responsibility has multiple benefits. Users will be better able to contribute to the overall security of the system with a good understanding of the things they need to be wary of and the things they need to do.

Looking Ahead

Many of the current problems with 802.11 protocols stem from design issues. WEP suffers from cryptographic design problems. Access points were designed to act as layer 2 bridges to facilitate roaming, which opened the network up to extensive ARP attacks. The focus on ease of use and quick setup has led to manuals that don't mention key security issues or safe configurations. As these issues have been brought to light, products have improved. Much work still needs to be done.

The newer 802.11 variants, such as 802.11a and the forthcoming 802.11g, attempt to address the shortcomings of 802.11b, providing improved bandwidth and security fixes. These changes will take time to mature, and will likely initially have some problems as well. However, security experts now are much more interested in the investigation of security problems in 802.11, so problems should be examined much more deeply.

The 802.11 family of protocols will continue to grow rapidly in both industry and the consumer market. It provides convenience for users and is affordable. Anyone who has worked from a wireless laptop understands how much less of a hassle it is compared to dealing with network cables strung all over.

Another strong driving force of the advancement of wireless technology is how hackable, in the good meaning of the word, 802.11 devices are. Many groups have sprung up that are attempting to use this equipment in novel ways. Some notable examples are the creation of mesh networks out of clusters of access points, loading Linux onto off the shelf access points to extend their functionality and the development of software like *HostAP*, which extends the capabilities of the hardware beyond the manufacturers intentions.

Unfortunately, wireless networks are also very hackable, in the bad meaning of the word. War drivers seek out vulnerable systems for exploitation from the wireless side, while all the usual suspects on the Internet probe the network from the other side. This increased risk and all the security issues discovered in 802.11 during 2001 created a media flurry of negative articles about wireless security. But, it seems, at least from our personal experience, that the benefits far outweigh the risks in most peoples minds. Many people realize there are security dangers and choose to set up a wireless network anyways since the convenience is worth much more to them than the possible compromises they might suffer.

In this book, we have presented a basic, practical approach to building small and medium sized wireless networks. Follow the instructions in this book, read the web sites of vendors and community wireless networks to learn about new threats and protections, and keep your software and drivers up to date.

Index

We'd like to hear your suggestions for improving our indexes. Send email to *index@oreilly.com*.

M

MAC address filtering
  access point security, 93
  impact on users, 165
  Linux gateways, 126
MAC addresses, limiting, 107
MAC (Media Access), 10
  address filtering (see MAC adress filtering)
  structure of 802.11 MAC, 12
Mac OS X
  auditing logs, 85
  client setup, 75–78
    AirPort access point utilities, 78
    card configuration, 75–78
    kernel configuration, 75
  operating system protection, 78–85
    disabling unneeded services, 78
    firewall configuration, 78–84
    static ARP, 84
  station security, 75–85
mail clients, supporting IMAP or SMTP over SSL, 35
mailing lists, xiii
man in the middle (see MITM attacks)
Management Information Base (MIB), 95
manipulating MITM attacks, 27
Media Access (see MAC)
MIB (Management Information Base), 95
MIB tree, walking, 96
Microsoft
  security patches, 86
  security resources, 86
  support for 802.1x protocol, 160
MITM attacks (man-in-the-middle attacks), 24–27
  eavesdropping, 25
  manipulating, 27
  static ARP, 47
MITM (man in the middle—see MITM attacks)
mixed environments, 94

N

NAT (Network Address Translation)
  OpenBSD gateways, 144
nat.conf, 144
Netfilter, 59
  configuration options, 54
  documentation, xiii
  enabling for Linux gateway, 118
  firewall rules for Linux gateway, 120–126
  firewall rules for Linux gateway, resources for, 126
net-snmp monitoring tool, 96
NetStumbler, 27
Network Address Translation (see NAT)
Network Properties control panel, 86
network-layer DoS attacks, 20
NoCat portal, 149

O

Object Identifier (OID), 95
OFDM (Orthogonal Frequency Division Multiplexing), 11
OID (Object Identifier), 95
omni-directional antennas, 6
open networks, 94
OpenBSD
  auditing logs (see FreeBSD, auditing logs)
  BIND and, 146
  client setup, 66–72
  firewall, 68
  gateway building, 139–147
    auditing logs, 147
    configuring NAT, 144
    DHCP, 146
    DNS, 146
    firewall rules, 141–144
    kernel configuration, 140
    service configuration, 140
    static ARP, 147
  kernel configuration, 66–72
    card configuration, 69–71
    security kernel, 68
    startup configuration, 71
    wireless kernel, 67
  kernel security levels, 141
  limiting traffic rates, 144–146
  operating system protection, 72–74
    disabling unneeded services, 73
    firewall configuration, 72
    static ARP, 73
  portability of, 67
  Principle of Least Privilege, 67
  securing access point, 106
  security vulnerabilities, resource for, 139
  setting up access point, 104–108
    HostAP configuration, 104
    startup files, 106
  station security, 66–74
  WiCap portal, 150

Windows
  auditing logs, 88
  client setup, 86
  file sharing on, 87
  operating system protection, 86–88
    firewall, 87
    static ARP, 87
    virus protection, 87
  station security, 86–88
Windows 2000, NSA guides for securing, 86
Windows 95/98, lack of security in, 86
Windows ME, lack of security in, 86
Windows NT, NSA guides for securing, 86
Windows Update tool, 86
Windows VPN clients, firewalls and, 87
Wired Equivalent Privacy (see WEP)
wireless, 4
  (see also radio transmission)
Wireless Application Protocol (WAP), 4
wireless DoS attacks, 21–24
  802.11b data-link, 22
  802.11b networks, 24
  802.11b physical, 21

Wireless Ethernet Compatibility Alliance (see WECA)
Wireless Fidelity (see Wi-Fi)
wireless interface driver types, 39
Wireless Local Area Networks (see WLANs)
Wireless Markup Language (WML), 4
wireless standards, 4
Wireless Transport Layer Security (WTLS), 4
wireness networks (see WLANs)
WLANs (Wireless Local Area Networks), 3
  performance of, 3
  reasons for deploying, 4
  risks, 3
  security of, 8
    (see also security)
  signal strength of, 6
WLCACHE option (FreeBSD), 40
WLDEBUG (FreeBSD), 40
WML (Wireless Markup Language), 4
WTLS (Wireless Transport Layer Security, 4

X

xinetd services, disabling, 119

About the Authors

Bruce Potter is Manager of Network and Security Operations for the Mass Markets Division of VeriSign. Trained in computer science at the University of Alaska Fairbanks, Bruce served as a senior technologist at Internet Alaska and Cigital prior to his work at VeriSign. He is founder and President of Capitol Area Wireless Network, a nonprofit based in Washington, DC. CAWNet, an organization of community members and commercial wireless Internet Service Providers (WISPs), is attempting to create a large-scale public wireless network throughout the metro-DC area. In 1999, Bruce founded The Shmoo Group, an ad hoc group of security professionals scattered throughout the world. Bruce's interests include wireless security, large-scale network architectures, open source software assistance, and promotion of secure software engineering. In his spare time, Bruce enjoys woodworking and listening to the Grateful Dead.

Bob Fleck is the Director of Methodology Development at Secure Software, Inc. His discussions on wireless security-related issues have been quoted in major media publications such as CNN and *The Wall Street Journal* and were presented at the IIS WiFi Forum in early 2002. In addition to his interest in network security, Bob researches and consults on the design and implementation of secure applications. Bob studied computer science at Case Western Reserve University in Cleveland, Ohio, and is a member of CAWNet and The Shmoo Group.

Colophon

Our look is the result of reader comments, our own experimentation, and feedback from distribution channels. Distinctive covers complement our distinctive approach to technical topics, breathing personality and life into potentially dry subjects.

The animal on the cover of *802.11 Security* is an Indian ringnecked parakeet. Indian ringnecked parakeets are native to northern Africa and India, but are kept as pets all over the world. They get their name from the distinct black ring that males develop upon reaching maturity.

Though Indian ringnecked parakeets are usually green, breeders have been able to produce blue, yellow, and albino mutations. Their beaks are dark coral on top and black underneath. The birds can reach between 16 and 20 inches from the top of their heads to the tips of their long tails.

These parakeets are very playful and require a lot of attention when kept in captivity. They can learn to talk and are talented whistlers. When treated well and kept active, they can live up to 30 years.

Darren Kelly was the production editor, Maureen Dempsey was the copyeditor, and Jan Fehler was the proofreader for *802.11 Security*. Nancy Crumpton provided production services and wrote the index. Linley Dolby and Claire Cloutier provided quality control.

Emma Colby designed the cover of this book, based on a series design by Edie Freedman. The cover image is a 19th-century engraving from the Dover Pictorial Archive. Emma Colby produced the cover layout with QuarkXPress 4.1 using Adobe's ITC Garamond font.

David Futato designed the interior layout. This book was converted to FrameMaker 5.5.6 with a format conversion tool created by Erik Ray, Jason McIntosh, Neil Walls, and Mike Sierra that uses Perl and XML technologies. The text font is Linotype Birka; the heading font is Adobe Myriad Condensed; and the code font is Lucas-Font's TheSans Mono Condensed. The illustrations that appear in the book were produced by Robert Romano and Jessamyn Read using Macromedia FreeHand 9 and Adobe Photoshop 6. The tip and warning icons were drawn by Christopher Bing. Linley Dolby wrote the colophon.